THE *TAXI* BOOK

THE TAXI BOOK

The Complete Guide to Television's Most Lovable Cabbies

JEFF SORENSEN

St. Martin's Press
New York

Design by John Fontana

Library of Congress Cataloging-in-Publication Data

Sorensen, Jeff.
    The Taxi book.

    Summary: Discusses the production, writing, cast, and 114 episodes of the successful television show, still enjoying popularity in syndication.
    1. Taxi (Television program) [1. Taxi (Television program) 2. Comedy programs. 3. Television programs] I. Title.
PN1992.77.T38S6   1987   791.45′72   87-4509
ISBN 0-312-00691-8 (pbk.)

First Edition
10 9 8 7 6 5 4 3 2 1

I would especially like to thank Ian Praiser, Barry Kemp, Michael Zinberg, Katherine Green, Randall Carver, and Jeff Conaway for all their help while I was doing the research for this book.

CONTENTS

THE *TAXI* BOOK

The original cast of *Taxi*

How *Taxi* Became a Hit TV Series

Viewers may imagine that selling a network on a new series would be a Herculean chore. We might envision months, if not years, of back-room pitches and deals, of desperate attempts to convince reluctant TV bigwigs that the series can't help but be a huge hit. (Perhaps a touch of bribery or blackmail would also be called for.) Selling the initial concept for *Taxi*, on the other hand, consisted only of the producers calling ABC and asking, "How about Judd Hirsch as a typical New York cabbie?"

The reason why the initial concept for *Taxi* was so easy to sell was that the four producers—James Brooks, Stan Daniels, David Davis, and Ed. Weinberger—who came up with the idea for the show had such an excellent track record. These men had all been writers and producers for *The Mary Tyler Moore Show*, and network executives felt confident that anything they did would attract an audience.

In more ways than one, *Taxi* is a descendant of *The Mary Tyler Moore Show*. Not only did many of the writers, pro-ducers, and directors of *Taxi* once work on *Mary Tyler Moore*, but it was *Mary Tyler Moore* that began the trend towards more realism in TV comedy when it premiered in 1970. What the creators of *Taxi* planned to do was to continue that trend, only in a completely different setting and with a completely different set of characters.

James Brooks remembers that "Dave Davis, who did *The Bob Newhart Show* [which was also produced by Mary Tyler Moore Enterprises], and I had the idea of doing a show about taxi drivers several years before we actually did it. We were going to do it with a writer named Jerry Belson. But he pulled out and we decided not to go ahead because we didn't have the time to devote to it . . . Then we formed this company [the John Charles Walters Company] with Ed. Weinberger and Stan Daniels, and Dave and I said, 'For our first project let's do the taxi idea.'"

Taxi was produced for ABC by Paramount in association with the John Charles Walters Company. Regular viewers of *Taxi* will recall that at the end of the credits following each episode, a harried-looking man walks down a hallway while a woman's voice calls after him, "Good night, Mr. Walters"; the man then responds with a groan. In reality, though, there is no such person as John Charles Walters. (The groan at the end of the credits is actually the voice of Ed. Weinberger.) Brooks, Daniels, Davis, and Weinberger used the fictitious name because they felt it sounded dignified. "We didn't want to use an amalgram of our names," remembers Weinberger. "We wanted something more distinguished. If there hadn't been a Robert Stigwood Organization, we would have loved that name. Then one day I saw a sign [at] an English pub that said 'Charles Walters.'"

Weinberger bought the sign, called his partners to tell them what he'd done, and received their approval to adopt the name for their company. He ordered stationery to be printed up. "Then I got a telephone call from a Charles Walters, a famous movie director who did *Singin' in the Rain* and *High Society*," says Weinberger. "His lawyers advised him it would not be a good idea to have a company with his name on it that he wasn't connected with in any way. So there we were—with a sign we couldn't use, obsolete stationery, and no name for our company. To avoid a lawsuit, we finally decided to call it the John Charles Walters Company."

The creators of *Taxi* visited several cab companies in New York while doing research for the pilot episode. "The whole

One of the best ensembles of performers ever put together for a sitcom, shown here in a first-season episode of *Taxi*.

show came together at five in the morning," recalls James Brooks. "Dave Davis and I were having coffee with New York's only charismatic cab driver, who came in and dropped off his cab. Two girls were waiting for him, and all the other cab drivers wanted to be with him. Everybody was saying how they intended to become actors and singers, and we said to him, 'What about you?' And he said, 'Me, I'm just a cab driver.' That gave us the key to Judd's character."

An article on cabbies by Mark Jacobson that appeared in *New York* magazine (the issue dated June 21, 1976) helped to suggest the idea of doing a show about taxi drivers to James Brooks and David Davis. Although nothing from the article, not even a line, was ever used on *Taxi*, the producers wanted to buy the rights to the article from Mark Jacobson. (It's a common practice in television to pay people whose work has helped in any way in the creation of a series.) "It turned out, though, that MTM already owned the option on the magazine article," recalls Weinberger. "But when we called, Grant Tinker [then the president of Mary Tyler Moore Enterprises] not only gave it to us, we got it for the original price—fifteen hundred dollars."

Brooks, Daniels, Davis, and Weinberger then got to work writing the script for the pilot episode. Brook says, "We were handed a blank check . . . on *Taxi* as far as giving writers and producers control over their work. The network did not interfere." From the beginning, explains Brooks, the producers planned for *Taxi* "to take on the day-by-day issues of living, of interpersonal relationships and heartbreak and disappointment and hopes and small dreams and big ones."

After they finished writing the script for the pilot episode (with Judd Hirsch in mind for the central character), the producers began to cast the leading roles during the spring of 1978. "They first talked to me before there was any kind of script, just an idea," says Hirsch. "Jim Brooks had talked to me about how *Taxi* would be a sitcom with a real acting ensemble. . . . But I told him 'no' when he approached me that first time. . . . Then I heard they were considering lots of other actors for the lead, including Tony Curtis, and I thought, 'If Tony Curtis is interested, it must really be something.' When they sent me the script, I read it and decided at once that I wanted the part. And it turned out to be everything they promised it would be."

Brooks remembers that "for Judd Hirsch we went to New York and really wooed. Danny DeVito walked into our office in character and was just really great; he came in as Louie DePalma. Marilu Henner we liked right away. Tony Danza I found in New York. Jeff Conaway had to read five times. Andy Kaufman we saw in concert at the Comedy Store, and we just went crazy and wrote a part for him to capture what he did."

The characters played by Marilu Henner and Tony Danza were different in the early drafts of the pilot script. Danza's character was originally supposed to be an Irish heavyweight, an older, punch-drunk fighter named Phil Ryan. Marilu Henner's character was supposed to be a tough-minded Italian woman in her thirties. But the producers changed the characters to fit the performers, because they were so impressed by their work. (Inci-

Latka Gravas and Elaine Nardo

dentally, the producers named Elaine Nardo and Tony Banta after the comedy-writing team of Pat Nardo and Gloria Banta, who formerly worked for Mary Tyler Moore Enterprises.)

With the leading roles finally set, the cast and crew of *Taxi* spent two weeks rehearsing before they filmed the pilot. Interestingly, a number of scenes originally shot for the pilot were cut when it was telecast. Some of these scenes were used later. (John Burns's first encounter with Alex Rieger was one of these: it was included in the episode "Memories of Cab 804.") And some of the original footage from the pilot was never shown at all, such as a scene of Bobby Wheeler appearing in a production of *Equus*. There was simply too much material for one episode in the original script for the pilot, yet the

producers felt it would be risky to begin a series with a two-part show. For that reason, the first episode of *Taxi*, "Like Father, Like Daughter," focused mainly on Alex and his relationship with his daughter, Cathy. The producers decided not to let the audience know much about some of the other regular characters until a few episodes later.

Taxi was first broadcast on September 12, 1978, and it was immediately well received by both viewers and critics. Tom Shales, a reviewer for the *Washington Post*, wrote, "*Taxi* is an enormously promising new series. . . . The quality of the dialogue on the premiere is particularly good —not just rapid-fire gags or exchanges but lines that delineate characters and states of mind."

"*Taxi* looks like a winner," said a reviewer for the Seattle *Post-Intelligencer.* "It has the writing, the actors, and the potential to become that rare breed of human television comedy that grows from people and not punchlines."

Within a few weeks the series moved into the top ten in the Nielsen ratings. (*Taxi* finished in tenth place in the Nielsens for the whole 1978–79 season.) The series stayed among the top-rated TV programs for most of its first three seasons. And *Taxi* won the Emmy Award for being the outstanding comedy series in each of those first three years.

During the fourth season, though, the ratings declined considerably. In fact, *Taxi* was down to 53rd place by the end of the 1981–82 season. (Part of the reason, surely, for this decline was that the show was moved in 1980 from a very favorable time slot, following *Three's Company* on Tuesday nights, to a shaky spot in the Wednesday-night schedule on ABC.) With such marginal ratings, it wasn't a great surprise when ABC announced the cancellation of the show in early 1982. "After ABC canceled *Taxi*," Tony Danza recalls, "we had a party all night. It was like a funeral, with a little taxi we put into a coffin. After a while we were having such a good time we almost forgot why we were partying and that we were all out of jobs."

But it wasn't the end; NBC picked up *Taxi* for a fifth season. The move to NBC in 1982 generated considerable attention in the press, especially since both NBC and Home Box Office made offers for the right to buy new *Taxi* episodes. NBC executives said they thought *Taxi* was a real feather in their cap. "By picking up the most acclaimed comedy on television, we feel we're sending out a signal that we're committed to high-quality programing," Brandon Tartikoff, president of NBC Entertainment, told the *New York Times.* In moving to NBC, the executive producers of *Taxi* were going back to work for their former boss, Grant Tinker, at that time the chairman of NBC, who had earlier been the president of Mary Tyler Moore Enterprises.

NBC received lots of congratulations for its decision to reprieve *Taxi*. In his column on television for the *New York Times*, Tony Schwartz wrote, "*Taxi* was perhaps the last three-dimensional show on ABC, which has virtually handed its prime-time schedule over to Aaron Spelling, the producer of such intellectual monuments as *The Love Boat, Fantasy Island*, and *Dynasty*. . . . NBC has picked [*Taxi*] up, taking a rare gamble on a good cause. Rooting for underdogs is almost always a noble enterprise, and in this case both *Taxi* and NBC qualify. Even if the show doesn't become a hit, Steve Sohmer deserves a raise. Mr. Sohmer is the new man in charge of promotion for NBC, and his whimsical spots for *Taxi* (and other NBC shows) may represent a breakthrough. They manage to celebrate television even as they poke gentle fun at it, and they are funny without the benefit of a laugh track." (The promos for *Taxi* that Schwartz referred to ended with Danny DeVito snarling, "Same time, better network.")

Despite these encouraging comments, the ratings for *Taxi* continued their downward slide on NBC (except in New York, where *Taxi* was always highly popular), and the last episode was telecast by NBC on July 20, 1983. The series remained a hit with the critics, though, right up to the end—and also with the Emmy Award voters. *Taxi* wound up with a total of fourteen Emmies, including awards in 1983 to Judd Hirsch for being the outstanding leading actor in a comedy series and to Christopher Lloyd and Carol Kane for being the outstanding supporting actor and actress in a comedy, variety, or music series.

Taxi went into syndication later in 1983, and since then it has regularly placed among the top twenty syndicated series in the Nielsens. Like many of the other programs that have developed a cult following over the years, *Taxi* seems to be continually attracting new audiences of viewers who hadn't watched the show regularly until it went into reruns. Besides the high quality of the series, another important reason, undoubtedly, for the good showing of *Taxi* in syndication is that quite a few members of the cast have gone on to other noteworthy series, movies, and plays.

CHAPTER 2

WHAT'S DIFFERENT ABOUT *TAXI*

After meeting a few other drivers on her first day of work for the Sunshine Cab Company, Elaine Nardo asks, "Why is everyone here just a little angry?" The answer, we soon discover, is that nearly everyone is putting in long hours at an unrewarding job and yearning for something better. Everybody seems to get on everybody else's nerves a lot of the time.

When Elaine, who also works at an art gallery, first meets Alex Rieger in the initial episode of *Taxi* ("Like Father, Like Daughter"), she is quick to say, "I'm only going to be working here part-time. . . . I'm not really a taxi driver." Alex nods his head and skeptically replies, "Oh yeah, I know. We're all part-time here. . . . You see that guy over there, now he's an actor. The guy on the phone, he's a prize fighter. This lady over here, she's a beautician. The man behind her, he's a writer. Me? I'm a cab driver. I'm the only cab driver in this place." Nearly all the cabbies, except Alex, have their own pipe dream of a better future. In fact, a typical episode of *Taxi* shows how one of the cab drivers goes after a new chance for success—only to return to the garage defeated for this time, but still hopeful about the future.

The special appeal of *Taxi* is that it features recognizable people instead of the wisecracking robots who populate most other sitcoms. The comedy in the series is derived from how the characters behave in believable circumstances; the show is not just a succession of one-liners and slapstick. (The only leading character in *Taxi* not at all based on reality is Latka Gravas, the cheerful mechanic from a mythical foreign country.) While the characters in a program like *The Honeymooners*, for example, always seem to be on stage, milking every joke for all it's worth, the characters in *Taxi* often seem to be caught unawares as they go about their day-to-day lives.

Because the cast of characters is based mainly on real people, the audience comes to care about what happens to each individual in a way that differs from how viewers react to most situation com-

An early publicity shot

edies. Instead of Martians or talking horses, the cast includes a middle-aged guy who's kindhearted but unambitious (Alex Rieger), a young divorced woman working at a job traditionally done by men (Elaine Nardo), a boxer who usually finishes each prize fight on the canvas (Tony Banta), an aspiring actor who can't seem to land a part anywhere (Bobby Wheeler), a burned-out former hippie (Jim Ignatowski), and an irredeemably nasty taxi dispatcher (Louie DePalma).

Since the comedy on *Taxi* is usually derived from real-life occurrences, the plots of many of the best episodes often sound more like drama than comedy. Wacky situations such as we see on shows like *I Love Lucy* or *Three's Company* are usually avoided on *Taxi*. (Viewers may remember, for instance, that Lucy was once locked into a room full of chimps. A scene like that would be hard to imagine on *Taxi*, as out of place as someone wandering into a posh nightclub wearing overalls.) The writers for *Taxi* resisted the temptation to clutter their scripts with gratuitous insults and wisecracks. Other sitcoms, though, are often full of not-too-bright characters who seem to have gag writers in their homes providing them with clever things to say. Most of the insult jokes on *Taxi* are saved for Louie, a character who would, in real life, say lots of insulting things to people. (Louie typically delivers such endearments as, "Banta, sometimes I wish you were smarter, just so you could see how dumb you are.") And many of the wisecracks are said by Alex, a guy who is smart enough to think them up. A character like Tony, on the other hand, is almost never given witty remarks; he's funny in other ways.

The meeting of Alex and his daughter, Cathy, in the first episode is a good example of the kind of humor that *Taxi* features. We learn that Alex hasn't seen Cathy in fifteen years; she's been living in Brazil with her mother, who has remarried. Alex discovers that Cathy will be stopping to change planes at the Miami airport on her way to attend college in Portugal, and he drives there with a few of the other cabbies in order to see her briefly. Alex finds the waiting area for her flight and looks around at the passengers. "If there's anything to genetics, I should be able to figure out which one she is," he says. He notices an attractive, dark-haired girl, walks over to her, and taps her on the shoulder:

Alex: Cathy Consuelos?

"I'm the only cab driver in this place," Alex tells Elaine on her first day of work.

Cathy: Yes?

Alex: I'm sort of your father.

Cathy: You're Mr. Rieger?

Alex: Right, Rieger. Right.

Cathy: Well, I've been wondering about you.

Alex: Yeah, same here. Would you like to sit down?

Cathy: Yes . . . I was always wondering what you looked like.

Alex: Well, I'm much better-looking than this. And you are very pretty.

Cathy: Thank you.

Alex: You're welcome. Hey, we're getting along great.

Cathy: How did you know I was going to be here?

Alex: Oh, fathers know these things. . . . Do you know anything about me? I mean, what have you heard?

Cathy: Just that you're living up on a ranch in Montana and you're thinking of running for United States Senate.

Alex: Uh, I've got some bad news for you—I lost the Senate race. No, I think your mother is trying to make me into much more of an exciting guy than I am. But the real story is almost as good: I'm a New York cab driver.

Throughout their talk father and daughter are a little awkward, unsure of what to say. After a few minutes Cathy appears to be getting irritated, and she tells Alex, "You keep on saying 'father,' but you're not my father. My father is a man who has raised me for as long as I can remember."

Alex replies, "Please don't tell me I don't remember the experience of having a daughter for two years. Please don't tell me that because I really do. I remember." She sees that he is sincere, and they part on friendly terms. As Cathy heads down the ramp to her plane, Alex gives her some final words of advice: "Don't trust guys who wear scarves. And don't trust guys who go too far down with the buttons on their shirt. And don't trust guys who wear too much religious stuff around their neck. . . . I mean, don't trust guys."

Another typical *Taxi* situation occurs in the episode "Elaine's Old Friend." Elaine picks up an old high school friend, Mary Parker, in her cab one night. Mary is extremely successful; she owns an advertising agency and she travels around the world with her boyfriend, an international lawyer. Elaine is so embarrassed about her life that she invents a story about an imaginary guy, a Columbia professor, who is supposed to be in love with her. The next day Elaine feels depressed. "I don't believe it," she tells Alex. "I'm ashamed of my own life." Elaine explains to the other cabbies that she and Mary were real competitors in high school. The other cabbies are sympathetic, but they tell her not to be upset.

Alex: Elaine, when you're a cab driver, it's a little natural to occasionally run into someone who's better off than you are.

Bobby: The people you run over are better off than you.

Jeff Conaway, who played the part of Bobby Wheeler, says, "It's kind of universal, the things we dealt with on *Taxi*. We dealt with the problems of relationships, the way you feel about yourself, how other people see you. Everything a human being deals with every day. And the writers were clever enough to get the point across and also make it funny."

Many of the situations on *Taxi* are concerned with friendship. (Lots of episodes—perhaps a few too many, in fact—end with people hugging.) "Friends," one of the best episodes of the series, is about Tony and Bobby's friendship. Tony and Alex are sitting in Bobby's apartment one evening talking about how forgetful and irresponsible Bobby is:

Tony: You take Bobby. He treats me

creepy. He ignores me. He calls me stupid. I mean, what do I like him for? There are guys I don't even like who treat me better. One guy I hate treats me almost as good.

Alex: I don't know what makes people friends, Tony.

Tony decides that he can't expect Bobby to be anything but what he is, unreliable. "If a guy doesn't do what he can't do, what you gonna do?" says Tony. "Friends" handles this situation nicely, without falling into the trap of becoming sentimental.

In his book *Cult TV*, John Javna offers

A typical *Taxi* scene at the Sunshine Garage

this accurate description of *Taxi:* "Louie is the Enemy, and the cabbies band together in mutual defense against him. But their relationship goes deeper than that. Without each other, these dreamers would be alone in life. So they tolerate each other's quirks, soothe each other's wounds, and celebrate each other's victories together. *Taxi* is a comedy about friendship—about people helping and needing each other."

Ian Praiser, one of the producers of *Taxi,* points out that "the show brought together characters who wouldn't normally be friends at all. I mean, would someone like Elaine have picked somebody like Tony for a friend if they didn't work together?"

"The essence of any good show," explains Mary Tyler Moore, "is the family relationship of the players. . . . Not blood relations necessarily, but the nucleus of people who fight with each other, love each other, and make up." The characters on *Taxi,* much like the characters on *The Mary Tyler Moore Show,* do form a sort of substitute family. Many of the characters on *Taxi,* such as Alex and Reverend Jim, are estranged from their real families. Bobby's father died when he was six years old. Elaine rarely mentions her parents. Louie and his mother are always fighting. So it seems only natural that, for the cabbies at the Sunshine Garage, the people they know at work have become their family. (And if the *Taxi* crew is a family, then we would have to say that Alex and Elaine are the parents; Tony, Jim, Bobby, and Latka are the children; and Louie is, possibly, a bad-tempered uncle. But would anyone admit that Louie was a part of his family?)

No other sitcom has ever featured the number and variety of clearly defined and memorable characters that we see on *Taxi;* the viewer feels happy to be spending time in the company of these people. While other series usually feature three or four main characters, *Taxi* has seven: Alex, Elaine, Louie, Tony, Bobby, Jim, and Latka. More important, the leading characters on *Taxi* are all of relatively equal importance. This gives a feeling of greater variety to the series. On the other hand, a series like *The Bob Newhart Show* focuses most of the time on just two characters, Bob and Emily. Even on *The Mary Tyler Moore Show,* which has an especially fine ensemble, almost all the episodes are concerned mainly with Mary, Lou, or Rhoda. Judd Hirsch is not the star of *Taxi* in the sense that, say, Bill Cosby or Bob Newhart are the stars of their current series.

The quality of the acting lifts *Taxi* above the level of most sitcoms. On paper, the basic setting of any one situation comedy looks much like any other. After all, there have been dozens of sitcoms set in the workplace in recent years. It's the details of acting and writing that set one series apart from another. And much of the acting on *Taxi* (especially that of Judd Hirsch) is more subtle, with a more perceptive feeling for realism, than we usually see on TV. In putting together the ensemble of actors for *Taxi,* the producers chose a group of performers who not only worked together smoothly but who could make their characters seem like people out of the everyday world. Even the best-written shows, like *Taxi* or *Mary Tyler Moore,* occasionally have weak scripts with some jokes that fall flat or

The quality of the acting lifts *Taxi* above the level of most sitcoms.

seem overfamiliar, but a strong cast is able to carry the audience past these shortcomings. One tribute to the excellence of the acting on *Taxi* is that the entire cast was nominated for a Golden Globe Award in 1979. Another sign of the high quality of the performers is that the members of the cast of *Taxi* have gone on to appear in a long and impressive list of television, movie, and theatrical projects since the show went off the air in 1983.

Besides the acting and writing, one other reason that *Taxi* conveys a strong feeling of being based on reality is that it is set in New York. Most sitcoms could take place in Anytown, U.S.A., but what happens on *Taxi* could only take place in Manhattan. The hectic pace of life and the diversity of the people there are an integral part of the show's appeal. Many of the characters, like Louie, the mean-spirited dispatcher, would seem out of place anywhere else but in New York. (In

the first episode, as soon as Louie finds out that Elaine has come to the garage not as a customer but to become one of his employees, he snarls at her, "You're a cab driver? What do ya mean bustin' my chops here, makin' believe you're a regular person? Go wait over there, I'll call your name and number—till then keep your mouth shut. . . . Fill out this form. And I hope you fill it out better than you fill out your pants.")

Another bit of realism on *Taxi* is that we're not given any false sense of optimism about the characters' chances for success. We don't feel that they're going to (in the words of the *Mary Tyler Moore* theme song) "make it after all." In a way, Louie is perfectly correct when he calls everybody in the garage a "loser." And Alex is, unfortunately, right to think that the future is probably not going to be a dream come true for most of the cabbies. For instance, when Alex hears that the Sunshine Cab Company has gone bankrupt (in "On the Job, Part I"), he says, "Maybe it's time to get out of the hack business. Maybe it's time for us to shed these old, lousy, nowhere jobs and find new, lousy, nowhere jobs." (As it turns out, though, the cabbies don't need to find jobs elsewhere because a new owner is found for the cab company.) Still, it should be pointed out that while the characters on *Taxi* can be described as "failures" in one sense (their "real" careers don't take off), they are successful in a more important sense—they are (with the exception of Louie) warm and compassionate people.

What makes *Taxi* different from other sitcoms, then, is that most of its characters are drawn from real life, that the humor is frequently subtle and assumes a level of sophistication and intelligence on the part of the audience, and that the scripts and performances are filled with innumerable touches of realism. Furthermore, the characters' pursuit of their pipe dreams about a better tomorrow gives a kind of theme to the whole series.

CHAPTER 3

ALEX RIEGER

Alex Rieger (portrayed by Judd Hirsch) is at the center of most of what happens on *Taxi*. He has been driving a cab for much longer than anyone else in the garage. And since he's also older than the other cabbies, it's only natural that they look up to him as something of an authority figure.

Alex is kindhearted. In fact, he's often too compassionate for his own good—he always seems to wind up trying to solve everyone else's problems. Louie often kids Alex for being such a good Samaritan. Here is one of their typical exchanges (from "Simka's Monthlies"):

Louie: Boy, Rieger, I'd hate to be you. I'd hate to be the one who ends up having to help everybody else. Geez, what a sap.
Alex: It may surprise you, Louie, but I happen to enjoy helping people. And, yes, I will admit, it gives me a certain pleasure.

(What Alex says here is totally lost on Louie, who shakes his head in disgust at what Alex tells him.)

When Louie and Alex are talking, it often seems as if they might as well be speaking different languages. There's just no way for compassionate Alex to really understand anyone as amoral as Louie. For instance, in a scene from the episode "Crime and Punishment," Louie and

Alex Rieger is sometimes too compassionate for his own good.

Alex are alone in the garage one night after Louie has just gotten away with lying and stealing; Louie is puffing on a cigar, guiltlessly enjoying the fruits of his crimes:

Louie: Rieger, you gotta help me. Explain to me what it's like to be honest. I mean, because, if I had a chance to do that all over again, I'd like to know one reason why I shouldn't.

Alex: I can't explain the feeling I get from being honest. It's like trying to explain April in Paris. You can't understand it unless you've been there.

In this scene Louie has an answer for Alex, although it's hardly one that Alex could sympathize with. Louie says, "Oh, I understand April in Paris. It's like having Havana cigars, a great drink of booze, and being off scot-free. That's April in Paris, Rieger. . . . You know, people go around thinkin' that if they do something bad, then something bad has got to happen to them. Well, I'm livin' proof that that is not true."

Alex prides himself on being a realist, a person who accepts things the way they are. As Judd Hirsch says, "Alex does not embellish life with would-be's and could-be's." Unlike the other cabbies, who all dream that one day they will become rich and famous, Alex realizes that he'll probably never be successful.

Yet Alex wasn't always like that. He tells a theatrical producer (in "Alex the Gofer") that "when I was younger, I wanted to work in the theater. I'd have done anything just to get my foot in the door." In another episode ("The Road Not Taken, Part II"), we see that Alex once had a chance to be promoted to the position of regional manager of a big company. He couldn't put up with the bootlicking behavior that his supervisors expected of him, however—and he quit. Ever since, he's never really tried to become successful, even though he is clearly an intelligent and capable man.

As one who has given up on many of his youthful dreams, Alex definitely has a morose side to his character. When Elaine tells him how wonderful a trip to Europe would be (in "Vienna Waits"), Alex replies, "It has been the lesson of my life that nothing that sounds *that* good ever really happens." When a new woman cabbie, seemingly overflowing with youthful high spirits, asks him for a date (in "Nina Loves Alex"), he tells Elaine, "The last thing I need in my life is a born-again cheerleader who's going to try to kick some life into the old boy."

Alex was divorced from his ex-wife Phyllis at a time when their daughter, Cathy was only two years old. (Alex caught Phyllis cheating on him.) He didn't see Cathy again until she was seventeen. And when Alex sees his own father in one *Taxi* episode, it's the first meeting of father and son in thirty years.

Alex seems never to have much luck romantically, and he's become a little cynical about his chances of falling in love again. We're introduced to a number of appealing women who Alex goes out with at one time or another, yet none of these relationships appears to last for long. He seems to be afraid of getting involved again, and he doesn't have much confidence that he is attractive to women.

Alex Rieger

Taxi is a long one. There's an episode ("Alex Gets Burned by an Old Flame") in which he becomes intrigued by a beautiful lawyer, Diane MacKenna, but she's more interested in Reverend Jim than in Alex. Another time (in "The Shloogel Show"), Alex pays a lot of attention to Susan McDaniels, an attractive woman whose sense of humor matches his own. He tells her, with real sincerity, "Somehow, I forgot what it was to feel the way I feel now about meeting somebody new." But Susan is reluctant even to give him her phone number. When Alex is about to ask a lovely soap opera actress, Joyce Rogers, to marry him (in "Alex's Romance"), she says, "God, I hope this isn't a proposal." "My heavens, no," Alex tells her, as he tries to act glib to cover up his disappointment, "this is my way of running for governor, and I was about to ask you for your vote." Although Alex and his ex-wife Phyllis once enjoyed a hot romance, she eventually grew tired of him because he was, in her words, "a failure." (She wanted him to get a better-paying job than that of a taxi driver.)

Even the way that Alex walks—he often looks tired and he has a ramshackle slouch—shows a lack of conviction in himself. The thought of Alex briskly and confidently striding into a room seems hard to imagine.

The list of his romantic setbacks on

Lack of ambition probably is Alex's biggest fault. As he says, "My shorts are more ambitious than I am." In fact, Alex is the first to make fun of his lack of aspirations. He points out that "one thing about being a cabbie is that you don't have to worry about being fired from a good job." A wealthy lady once asks him, "What do you do?" To which Alex replies, "I just drive a cab." Then she asks, "What do you want to do?" "Quit," he says.

One of Alex's main activities on *Taxi*, it seems, is lending support to the other cabbies' efforts to improve themselves. They know that they can count on him to give them confidence in themselves or to cheer them up after they've taken a fall. (Maybe this is Alex's way of compensating himself for his own lack of self-confidence.)

Alex's sensitivity toward other people marks him as similar in some ways to the leading male characters of other memorable TV series of the late seventies and early eighties. Hal Linden on *Barney Miller,* Alan Alda on *M*A*S*H,* Daniel J. Travanti on *Hill Street Blues,* and Ed Asner on *Lou Grant* played men who had much in common with Alex Rieger. The characters these men portrayed all prided themselves on treating others fairly, and they didn't play the part of the tough, "macho" leading man. In the past few TV seasons, though, there seems to be a trend away from these more "sensitive" types and a return to more traditional, aggressive leading men. Although Captain Furillo of *Hill Street Blues* and Alex Rieger of *Taxi* always treat women with tenderness, the male stars of *Miami Vice* and *Moonlighting* are very different. Ted Danson's character, Sam, on NBC's *Cheers* (created by several former producers of *Taxi*) is another example of this recent trend: he's known as a womanizer who makes a play for every attractive girl he meets. It is hard to picture Alex Rieger seducing a girl casually and then dumping her. We'd imagine that he couldn't live with himself after doing something like that.

At times, Alex can be almost maddeningly sane. Usually he is very even-tempered and keeps a firm rein on his im-pulses. And since he is normally so much in control of his emotions, some of the most interesting episodes are those in which he faces a truly difficult choice or is especially aroused by something he can't just shrug off.

For example, in the episode "Alex Tastes Death and Finds a Nice Restaurant," Alex's ear is nearly shot off in a holdup attempt in his taxi. He is so upset that he astonishes everybody by quitting the Sunshine Cab Company . . . for a while. In "Alex's Romance" he becomes so enamored of Joyce Rogers that he asks her to marry him, even though they had agreed not to become seriously involved. "Alex Goes Off the Wagon" shows him at the lowest point of the whole series. Here we learn that Alex is a compulsive gambler. We see him looking disheveled as he desperately tries to borrow money from Jim, something Alex would normally never even consider doing, in order to support his gambling habit.

But Alex's most dramatic moment is in the episode "Alex Jumps Out of an Airplane," when he briefly becomes a daredevil. To impress a woman, Alex actually goes off a ski jump, although he's never jumped before and isn't even much of a skier. All the other cabbies are speechless when he tells them, "That was the biggest thrill of my life. Ever since that Saturday and that ski jump . . . my food has tasted a little better, the air has smelled a little fresher, the sky seems a little bluer, and this life has seemed just a little bit nicer. So, I've decided the most important thing in a man's life is to face his fears." Of course, he doesn't succeed in transforming himself, but we're pleased to know that Alex, who's often so melancholy, has enjoyed such a thrilling experience.

Alex is, above all, a well-rounded, life-like character whose shortcomings only serve to make him more appealing. To most of us, Alex is someone who we feel we would want to know and who, we hope, would want to know us.

THE REST OF THE REGULAR CAST

ELAINE NARDO

The chemistry between Elaine Nardo (played by Marilu Henner) and Alex—and their growing respect for each other—is central to the appeal of the show. Elaine and Alex are much more sensible than the other characters: they're both well-balanced people. Elaine and Alex are the ones the other characters turn to when they need help. If the *Taxi* crew is a family, then Elaine and Alex are the parents (though Elaine would certainly be repelled at the notion of being in any way related to Louie). Marilu Henner says, "I like Elaine. She and Alex are the most intelligent, sane people among the regulars on *Taxi*. Elaine isn't one of your dumb TV broads." Elaine and Alex sleep together only once; both say they ended their affair because they didn't want to spoil their friendship. According to Alex,

Elaine Nardo keeps the series from being almost totally dominated by the male point of view.

The chemistry between Elaine and Alex is central to the appeal of the show.

"People who work together shouldn't get involved." But even though their relationship isn't usually romantic, we sense that Elaine and Alex are at least as deeply involved in each other's lives as lovers would be.

Many of the best episodes of the series focus on Elaine and Alex together. In "Come as You Aren't," Elaine pleads with Alex to forgive her for making him lie to some stuffy art-world people about what he does for a living. In "Elaine's Old Friend," Alex pretends to be passionately in love with Elaine in order to impress Mary Parker, who knew Elaine from high school. And in "Vienna Waits," Elaine and Alex finally consummate their attraction for each other. In a fancy restaurant

on the last night of their trip to Europe together, Elaine says, "Alex, we've known each other for four years now. We've seen each other depressed, neurotic, sad, angry, hostile, stupid, ugly—and yet we've still remained friends. Maybe our friendship is strong enough to survive one night of love."

Besides not wanting to ruin their friendship, another reason, probably, that Elaine and Alex don't continue their affair is that both of them have become a little cynical about romance and are afraid of getting hurt again. "Romance never works out," Elaine says. "Only in fiction . . . I want to live in fiction. And it doesn't even have to be *Wuthering Heights*." In the episode in which John

Burns gets married ("The Great Line"), we see Elaine sitting at Mario's looking depressed. "It's never gonna happen to me," she says. "I'm gonna spend the rest of my life alone . . . alone . . . alone." Another time (in "Memories of Cab 804, Part II"), Elaine picks up a fare who seems to be her ideal of the perfect man. He's named Mike Brandon, and he's good-looking, smart, courteous, and successful. Elaine tells him, "This is too perfect. Something's going to go wrong. I just know it's gonna turn out that you're married, gay, or crazy."

It isn't surprising that Elaine has grown skeptical about men and relationships, considering that her former husband, Vince, was something of a heel. (On several occasions she makes derogatory remarks about Vince. Elaine says that he was irresponsible and that he was a heavy gambler—which is why she sometimes lectures the other cabbies about the evils of betting on anything.) Furthermore, it's only natural that a woman as attractive as Elaine has heard every possible line from men, and so she tends to doubt what she's told.

Elaine had been divorced for only a few months when she joined the Sunshine Cab Company. On weekdays Elaine works as a receptionist at the Hazeltine Art Gallery, though she hopes one day to run a gallery of her own.

She worries a lot about being a good mother. Sometimes the pressures of holding down two jobs and being a single parent with two children, Jason and Jennifer, get to be almost too much for Elaine to cope with. At one point (in "Nardo Loses Her Marbles"), Alex even persuades her to visit a psychiatrist when she is over-whelmed by her impossibly busy routine. Elaine is reluctant to admit needing help, and she tells the psychiatrist, "There's nothing wrong with me. It's just that I have to prove to a certain person that I don't need any help." She says to the doctor, "I'm very organized. I have this very elaborate schedule. Sure sign of mental health, huh?"

Occasionally Elaine gets dejected, thinking that her life hasn't measured up to what she had once expected. In "Elaine's Old Friend," when she gives a taxi ride to her old high school friend Mary, who's fabulously successful, Elaine keeps insisting (so strongly that she gives herself away) that she's not embarrassed about her life. Elaine says, "Mary, you don't have to feel sorry for me . . . because there's no reason to . . . because I'm very happy."

Elaine's temper flares up sometimes, but usually only when she's provoked. The angriest that we ever see her is the time (in "Louie Goes Too Far") she discovers that Louie has been spying on her when she's in the ladies' room. She becomes enraged and gets someone from the National Organization for Women to come to the garage and threaten legal action against him. ("Might I suggest a spanking?" Louie replies.) Louie is then fired, and he has to beg Elaine to help him get his job back.

Like Alex, Elaine keeps her strongest emotions under control most of the time. She is the kind of person whom everyone else can depend on. Like Alex, she plays a sort of amateur social worker on *Taxi*, helping the other cabbies to get over their disappointments. And she keeps the series from being almost totally dominated by the male point of view.

"Louie's got a crusty exterior, but underneath there's a heart of granite."

LOUIE DEPALMA

Louie DePalma (played by Danny DeVito) has been the dispatcher at the Sunshine Cab Company for many years. He is the sort of guy who can almost make Attila the Hun look compassionate. He frequently makes fun of the other characters' ambitions; Louie thinks that everyone else in the garage is a "loser." "Only one guy ever made it out in the whole history of this garage," he says, "and that was James Caan. And *he'll* be back." Louie bets against Tony whenever he boxes. In fact, the only reason Louie is

dejected when he finds out that Tony's boxing license has been revoked (in "Out of Commission") is that it means he can't win any more money betting on Tony's fights.

But Louie's favorite target of abuse in the garage is Bobby. Regarding Bobby, Louie says, "When this guy's in a play, the highest-priced seats are near the exits." When Bobby comes back to New York after going out to Hollywood to try his luck in a TV pilot (in "Bobby Doesn't Live Here Anymore"), Louie greets him by saying, "Well, it's Bobby Wheeler, the great actor. If I'd a known you were comin', I'd a baked a ham. . . . Come to beg for your job back, huh, Bob?" After hearing several more insults about Bobby from Louie, Alex gets irritated.

Louie's favorite target of abuse is Bobby.

Louie DePalma is the sort of guy who can almost make Attila the Hun look compassionate.

Alex: If Bobby gets the part . . . you'll congratulate him in front of all of us.
Louie: Couldn't I just take out my appendix with a warm spoon?

Though Louie was a cab driver himself for over ten years, he now calls the cabbies "scum." Sometimes he even wraps a handkerchief around his hand when he pulls up one of the cabbies' chairs so that he won't have to touch something they've touched. DeVito does such a convincing job of portraying Louie as a mean-spirited guy that we feel we would never want to go near a taxicab garage. After all, somebody like Louie might be working there.

During his years as a cab driver, Louie apparently never made much money, although he was one of the better bookers in the garage. Because of his small earnings, he lived for years in shabby apartments and only owned one suit. "I always wanted a really great apartment," Louie says, "something plush: with the pipes inside the walls." With the extra money he gets from his dispatcher's salary and with a loan from Jim, Louie can afford a classy uptown co-op (in the episode "Louie Moves Uptown"). When he first goes to look at the co-op apartment, he's so excited by the luxury of the place that he gets down on the floor and wallows around in the thick carpeting.

At one point we discover that Louie has invested part of his money in a nursing home. He tries to operate the place by cutting corners on every expense. "Do they really *need* three meals a day?" he asks.

Some of the funniest moments of the show occur when Louie goes into one of his weird little dances for joy, during which he often clicks his heels together. He dances when he's feeling especially good—which usually means that one of the cab drivers has just proven himself a failure at something.

Only one other thing really makes Louie ecstatic: money. In "Alex Goes Off the Wagon," Alex loses some money gambling, while Louie wins. Louie then tells him, "I'd love to stay here and com-

Louie goes into one of his weird little dances for joy.

fort you. But I'd rather go home and lay all this money on my bed and get naked and roll around in it until it sticks to my sweaty body."

Louie's appearance is unrefined, to say the least. His hair is usually a mess, and his clothes are usually wrinkled. He is only five feet tall, and he is decidedly overweight. (When he jumps into the bed of Alex's ex-wife Phyllis and takes off his shirt, revealing his hairy, flabby chest, Phyllis remarks, "It's great to see someone who's not caught up in the exercise fad.") Louie's voice is hoarse and grating; when Jim hears it, he sometimes covers up his ears and grimaces. Often, when Louie is mad, he bares his teeth like an animal. When he's upset, he frequently mumbles incomprehensibly to himself. All of these quirky mannerisms are handled adeptly by Danny DeVito, whose acting on *Taxi* is marked by a real theatrical zest.

Louie is a man who is virtually redolent of shallow morals. He goes through all the drivers' lockers at the Sunshine Cab Company. He charges each cabbie a dollar just to take a phone message. He tells Latka to remember that "lust is better than love," and he makes sleazy remarks to nearly every woman he sees. Louie looks forward to apologizing as much as most people would look forward to swallowing a bone. He knows no shame in excessively flattering his bosses. And Louie just loves to deliver bad news. Alex is, of course, disgusted when this happens.

Alex: Why would anyone go out of his way to tell depressing news to another human being?
Louie: Kicks.

Louie calls everyone else in the garage a "loser."

Louie: Why can't you forgive me?
Elaine: Because you're not really sorry. Because you don't even understand what was wrong with what you did.
Louie: You mean, if I understood what was wrong with what I did, then you'd forgive me and get me my job back?
Elaine: But you won't understand. . . . In a way, I'm hoping that you really would understand this because I'd like to forgive you.
Louie: And I'd like to be forgiven. What's holding us up?

On innumerable occasions Louie shows us that he totally lacks sensitivity towards others. Here is how he handles an irate woman calling the garage to complain: "Ma'am, you say one of our drivers was rude to you? . . . What was it he said exactly? . . . I see. . . . And just how fat are you?"

Basically, Louie is one of those individuals with no real understanding of anybody else's feelings: he knows only his own self-interest, like a child. This exchange between Louie and Elaine, from the episode in which she finds out he has been spying on her in the ladies' room ("Louie Goes Too Far"), reveals his warped point of view.

Stan Daniels explains that "Louie's got a crusty exterior, but underneath there's a heart of granite." According to James Brooks, "There was a big struggle not to make him [Louie] nicer. The big struggle with him was not to give him that heart of gold." It's fortunate that Brooks was able to keep Louie from becoming more conventional. What is unique about Louie, for a main character in a sitcom, is that he is incurably nasty. The audience doesn't sense that he is merely acting tough in order to conceal his more tender emotions: we feel that he is hard all the way through, as Daniels says. And as a thoroughly mean-spirited guy, Louie serves as the perfect foil for the other characters on *Taxi*.

TONY BANTA

Tony Banta (portrayed by Tony Danza) is a fighter who's been knocked out so many times that the boxing commission revokes his license on the grounds that he is in danger of getting a concussion. Everyone on *Taxi*, including Tony, is

Tony Banta is a boxer who finishes most of his fights on the canvas.

Louie: Hey, Tony, you get creamed in your fight last night?

Tony: I didn't get creamed. I lost by a decision. (Tony walks away, then mutters) . . . The referee decided I was bleedin' too much.

Tony doesn't even own a robe until the other cabbies present him with one. (Tony Danza didn't have a robe early in his boxing career, either.) Previously, Tony Banta had gone into the ring with a Holiday Inn towel thrown over his shoulders.

In the episode "One-Punch Banta," Tony finally does get a shot at a major contender in a bout at Madison Square Garden. Before the fight Tony says, "I still can't believe I'm here. Ever since I'm fourteen, not a day goes by when I don't spend three hours in the gym. I thought I'd win the Golden Gloves. I didn't. I thought I'd win the Olympics. I didn't. I didn't even see the Olympics. My set blew out." Not surprisingly, Tony doesn't win his big fight at Madison Square Garden, either.

"Out of Commission" is the episode in which a doctor examines Tony, advises him to quit fighting, and finally takes Tony's case to the medical board. The state boxing commission revokes his license (because he may have suffered some brain damage), and he is despondent. "What am I gonna do? Boxing's my whole life," says Tony. In desperation, Tony decides to fight under an assumed name, Kid Rodriguez, and he has one more bout, which he loses by default, before the other cabbies convince him to stop.

Tony has been retired for about a year

aware that he's not one of the greatest boxers of all time. Tony's record before being forced to stop fighting was eight wins and twenty-four losses, with fourteen losses by knockout. His nose was broken six times. Louie always bets against him and calls Tony his "meal ticket." When we first meet Tony in the initial episode of *Taxi*, he's talking to Louie.

Tony Banta and Louie DePalma

when he meets Lucius Franklin, a positive-thinking pro football player (portayed by Bubba Smith), who gets Tony to reapply for his boxing license (in "Tony's Comeback"). Tony manages to get his license back and returns to boxing for the last one and a half seasons of *Taxi*.

Everyone (except Louie, of course) seems to like Tony, because he's such a sweet-tempered fellow. He has an infectious grin and he's boyishly shy. His personality is upbeat and he easily becomes enthusiastic. The few times we see him win a fight, he usually goes wild with excitement, jumping up and down and waving his arms.

Though likable, Tony Banta isn't terribly bright. Once he tells Alex, "Next week I have to take my college aptitude test. In my high school they didn't even teach aptitude." When Tony finds out that Bobby is touring in a role in *Under the Yum-Yum Tree*, Tony asks, "Isn't that *Desire Under the Yum-Yum Tree?*"

In "Fantasy Borough," when we learn what each of the cabbies fantasizes about, viewers see that Tony imagines himself picking up Eric Sevareid in a cab. And in Tony's fantasy, Sevareid is impressed with Tony's brilliant ideas on politics.

Sevareid: You seem to have a perspective on world events that somehow eludes the average man. . . . I just want you to come and be on my side in the debate.
Tony: Who're we debating?
Sevareid: Bill Buckley, Henry Kissinger, and John Kenneth Galbraith.
Tony: We'll kick their butts.

Tony assumes that his lack of sophistication will be a turn-off to women who are well bred. That's why some of his most poignant scenes are in "Tony's Lady." In that episode, Tony gets a job as a chauffeur for a rich girl, Christina. He tells the cabbies that he likes her a lot but that she is "out of my league." Yet he entertains her one night in the limousine with stories about his career as a fighter, and he says to Christina, "How about that? All these years of boxing finally paid off. I have amusing anecdotes." Tony seems pleased with himself for coming up with the phrase "amusing anecdotes."

Tony adopts a son, Brian (played by Tony Danza's son Marc), who figures in several episodes. They meet for the first time (in "The Reluctant Fighter") when Tony is about to fight an ex-champ who is coming out of retirement in order to win enough money for an operation that will enable Brian to walk again. Tony wins the bout, and he agrees to fight for Brian in the future.

In one of the last episodes, "Tony's Baby," Tony's girlfriend Vicki tells him she's pregnant. He offers to marry her, yet at first she flatly refuses him. We never find out for certain if they are to be married, but it appears likely that they would have been if *Taxi* had not been canceled so abruptly by NBC. Vicki and Tony seem like a good match: they're both outgoing, high-spirited, and down-to-earth people.

Like Vicki, most fans of *Taxi* have a special fondness for Tony Banta. He's so agreeable, so full of good intentions, that we can't help but respond warmly to him. In every way he is the exact opposite of Louie DePalma.

REVEREND JIM IGNATOWSKI

Reverend Jim Ignatowski (portrayed by Christopher Lloyd) is a minister of the "Church of the Peaceful." We're introduced to him during a first-season episode ("Paper Marriage") in which he marries Latka to an American girl. James Burrows, the director of many *Taxi* episodes, recalls, "We had guys reading for us doing drunks, evangelical preachers . . . but as soon as he [Christopher Lloyd] walked into the casting office, we just absolutely fell down. Everybody knew he was Reverend Jim, and we started talking the day after the taping about bringing him back the next year and getting him to be a cab driver."

"A character is written as a one-shot," says Ed. Weinberger, "and when you find the right actor to play it, the character just comes alive, and you're laughing from the first moment of rehearsals."

Late in the first season of *Taxi*, the John Burns character was dropped from the show, and the producers were looking for a replacement. Naturally, they thought of Reverend Jim.

"Lloyd came in the second season," says James Brooks. "We believed it was the right choice to make for the show. We didn't think the mix [of characters] was working. . . . The Chris Lloyd character I love; [he's the] only drugged-out character on television."

Lloyd's performance as Jim Ignatowski is a scathingly funny portrait of what happened to many of the flower children of the sixties. "I have a function in life; I stand for something," says Jim. "Not everybody stands for something, but I

Reverend Jim seems to have an almost infinite number of peculiarities.

do. I am the living embodiment of the sixties. Everything that came along, I went with. Even if I didn't know what it was, I went with it. . . . I dropped acid, I wore flowers in my hair, I went to Woodstock. . . . I marched and protested against that crummy war." As a result, Jim's thinking is none too clear after all those acid trips. Jim lived in a condemned building for four years. He accidentally set fire to Louie's apartment. For a while he lived in a 'sixty-three Volkswagen. And at one point, he even kept a broken-down racehorse named Gary in his apartment. For Jim, a simple question like "How are you doing today?" can be tough to answer.

When the *Taxi* gang helps him to get his hack's license (in "Reverend Jim: A Space Odyssey"), he is required to fill out an application. Bobby asks him a few questions from the form.

Bobby: Have you ever experienced loss of consciousness, hallucinations, dizzy spells, convulsive disorders, fainting, or periods of loss of memory?
Jim: Hasn't everyone?
Bobby: Mental illness or narcotic addiction?
Jim: That's a tough choice.

Reverend Jim seems to have an almost infinite number of peculiarities. His voice sounds like it has cobwebs in it. His diet consists mainly of Spaghetti-O's. He has

Jim's thinking is none too clear.

seen *E.T.* sixty-four times. He screams in his sleep. He can play Pac-Man for hours at a time. And the way that he moves is certainly odd: it's almost like watching another species—some kind of bird, perhaps. Jim's gestures tend to be abrupt. He'll look down, shake his head, and stretch out his arms horizontally. While sitting, he'll sometimes coil and uncoil his body, shooting out an arm, grabbing a knee, or mussing up his hair. After getting up for a few minutes, he may suddenly collapse into a chair as if thoroughly exhausted by the effort of standing.

Jim's appearance is not likely to remind anyone of Fred Astaire. Jim wears the same clothes for many days, if not

weeks, at a time. His hair is wildly unkempt and he shaves only intermittently: there's always a few days' worth of stubble on his face.

One of the biggest surprises of the series came when viewers discovered that Jim's father is fabulously wealthy. In one episode ("Going Home"), Alex and Jim go to visit Jim's family after a private investigator sent by his father finally locates him. We find out that Jim's real last name is Caldwell and that he once attended Harvard. At dinner in the Caldwell mansion, Jim and his father (played by Victor Buono) talk for the first time in years.

Mr. Caldwell: Jim was there [at Harvard] for a year. Got excellent grades one semester, and the next semester he wrote all his term papers in finger paint.

Jim: A typewriter seemed so impersonal.

Mr. Caldwell: I would seriously like to know what the past ten years of your life have consisted of. . . . What have you been doing with yourself? Drifting? Living on handouts? Getting stoned?

Jim: Well, don't make it seem so bad.

One of Jim's funniest scenes is in "The Road Not Taken, Part I." In that episode we get to see what he was like during his first semester at Harvard. Jim was then a model student. And he was meticulously neat. He enters his dorm room looking brushed, combed, and spotlessly clean. His girlfriend, Heather, attempts to convince him to try a marijuana brownie, but he resists her—for a while. "It's not just doing your own thing," he tells her, "it's doing the *right* thing. We're not here to party or to protest, but to learn. Who are going to be the leaders of tomorrow?" Certainly not the Jim we know from ten years later.

When Mr. Caldwell dies, he leaves a considerable part of his fortune to Jim, but Jim's relatives get a judge to declare him incompetent to receive the money (in "Jim's Inheritance"). However, the administrators of the Caldwell estate do send checks to Jim regularly as an allowance. With his extra money Jim buys Mario's, the cabbies' hangout, and by the end of the series, he is in the habit of frequently giving away a thousand dollars at a time to strangers.

Many viewers of the series name Reverend Jim as their favorite character on *Taxi*, and it's certainly true that there are lots of times when his quirky behavior and the strange things he says are irresistibly funny.

BOBBY WHEELER

The acting career of Bobby Wheeler (portayed by Jeff Conaway) rarely seems to get much past the auditioning stage, though he does eventually move to Hollywood, where (in the episode "Bobby Doesn't Live Here Anymore") he lands a role in a pilot for a new TV series called *Boise*. True to form for Bobby, the network executives decide to produce *Boise*, but they recast his part.

Conaway describes Bobby as "a bud-

The acting career of Bobby Wheeler rarely seems to get much past the auditioning stage.

Bobby's best friend in the garage is Tony.

ding actor whose talents have yet to be discovered. He's a real good actor. But he's not dedicated to a point where he'd rather starve than not act. He's constantly in conflict with trying to make it as an actor and wanting money. . . . Bobby is forgetful, a little scatterbrained, and he would give you the shirt off his back. In fact, he can take the shirt off your back and forget to return it to you. He's in his own world."

Bobby does manage to land a few acting jobs over the course of three seasons of *Taxi* episodes. Unfortunately, most of the roles he gets aren't in what could be called Tony Award material. For instance, he appears in an experimental play entitled *Stalled*, about a group of people getting stuck in an elevator.

In an episode early in the first season, "Bobby's Acting Career," Bobby tells the other cabbies, "When I first came to New York, I made this deal with myself. . . . I gave myself a strict time limit, three years. . . . I promised myself that in that amount of time if I didn't get a paid acting job, I'd give it up." The three-year deadline passes, but he decides to give himself another three years. And he does much better in those next three years, landing eight professional acting roles and several commercials. Still, the big break continues to elude him.

One of the times he gets closest to becoming a star is in "What Price Bobby?" At the beginning of this episode, Bobby is cruising the theater district in his cab, hoping to meet an important theatrical producer or agent. By a terrific stroke of luck, one of the most influential actors' managers in New York, Nora Chandliss, gets into his cab. He pitches her on his acting abilities, and she tells him she might come to Brooklyn and watch him in *Stalled*. After seeing the play she agrees to manage him. She gets Bobby a part in a major production of *Cat on a Hot Tin Roof*, but we discover that she's only helping him in order to be able to sleep with him. Bobby obliges once, and then he becomes increasingly uncomfortable with the arrangement. When he asks that their relationship be strictly professional, she drops him.

The situation in "What Price Bobby?" offers Louie a chance to get off some of his choicest put-downs. "Are you saying you're using your body to further your career?" Louie asks Bobby. "Now that is smart. I'm glad you finally figured it out that you're not gonna get there on your talent." Louie derives a great deal of satisfaction from hearing about Bobby's bad breaks. In fact, Louie can recite whole catalogues of insults about Bobby's acting skills: "I'm not sayin' that Bobby Wheeler's a bad actor, but the only one who ever waited for him backstage was the playwright—and he had a hammer." Another time Louie says, "If you held a gun to his head, Wheeler couldn't act nervous."

If Bobby's worst enemy in the garage is Louie, then his best friend is probably Tony. Tony's relationship with Bobby is featured in "Friends," which Conaway names as one of his favorite episodes. "Friends" tells about the time Tony becomes incensed with Bobby for letting his pet fish die. (In the end, Tony realizes

that if he wants to get along with Bobby, he has to accept the fact that Bobby is going to continue doing some irresponsible things.) And in "A Woman Between Friends," Bobby and Tony compete over a beautiful girl. Most of the time, though, they get along well; each tries to cheer the other up when one of them suffers another setback in his career—which is probably the reason they've remained friends.

Bobby has known his share of failures in his career, but he does have a well-earned reputation as a great success with women, who (except for Elaine) seem to find him irresistible. Elaine says to Bobby, "You don't pay attention to women, you collect them." Bobby instinctively puts the moves on every attractive woman he meets. For example, when Alex is preparing to take his first parachute jump and is absolutely terrified, Bobby sits with him on the plane—and still manages to flirt with the woman instructor. ("Couldn't you wait until I'm gone?" Alex asks.)

No one could accuse Bobby of being excessively humble. He has a rakish smile. He's very concerned about his appearance. He doesn't like anyone touching his hair, and he often tosses his head back arrogantly. Bobby is so pleased with what he sees in the mirror that he describes himself as "a great-looking guy." One time he says, "It's a handicap to be classically handsome." Conaway does a good job of conveying Bobby's conceit about his appearance. Bobby may be insecure about his abilities as an actor, but he feels totally assured that he's attractive to women.

That's why it comes as a real blow to

him when he finds out the reason he has been dropped from the *Boise* TV series: the producers claim he isn't sexy enough for the part. The gang attempts to revive his spirits, however, and he finally decides to go back to Hollywood and give acting another try. And we never see Bobby again.

Bobby Wheeler made an important contribution to the mix of characters on *Taxi*. On the one hand, Bobby has a lot of bad points: he's vain, self-centered, irresponsible, and sometimes scatterbrained. On the other hand, he usually means well, and he rarely does anything to hurt somebody else deliberately. (Compared with Louie, his motives are as pure as a saint's.)

Without Bobby, the last two seasons of *Taxi* aren't usually quite up to the standard of the first three, although many of the later episodes are still very funny. In the last two seasons, there are just too many crazy characters. Reverend Jim, Latka, and Simka are all interesting when considered individually, but having all of them as regulars on *Taxi* at the same time nearly shifted the balance away from the more normal characters like Alex and Elaine. It's too easy, in a way, to get laughs when the cast is filled with certifiable loonies. This change in the mix of the characters might have been one of the reasons that the ratings for the show declined after the first three seasons.

LATKA AND SIMKA GRAVAS

Latka Gravas (played by Andy Kaufman) and his wife Simka (played by Carol Kane) speak an unusual language that no one else in the garage can even begin to understand. It's a strange hodgepodge of different sounds and rhythms; Kaufman, who invented the language, said that it's a form of "glottal gobbledygook." Though we can figure out what some of the words stand for ("nik-nik," for instance, means making love), other words and phrases remain baffling. The expression "ibi da" seems to have dozens of different meanings—including "thank you," "I do," "please," "yes," and others.

Latka's mythical homeland, which is never named, seems to be very tiny and to have an even tinier population. (Simka is the only one from the country who speaks French.) The country is apparently located somewhere in central or eastern Europe. The customs of Latka's homeland are unusual, to say the least. He explains that "in my country everybody shares with everybody else—otherwise we shoot them." When Simka finds out that Latka has slept with a woman cab driver (in "Sceneskees from a Marriage"), a religious leader decrees that Simka in turn must sleep with someone else from the garage. (She picks Alex, but he declines.) Tradition in Latka's and Simka's country requires that a proposal of marriage can only be made by a type of marriage broker called a "gewirtzal." Whenever anyone offers money to someone from their culture, the person receiving it is supposed to protest vehemently—whether or not they intend to keep the money.

When we see Latka at work as the mechanic for the Sunshine Cab Company, he is usually in a chipper mood, unconcerned with whatever may be happen-

Latka and Simka Gravas speak a strange language that no one else in the garage can even begin to understand.

ing around him. In the early episodes of *Taxi*, Latka sticks mainly to the role of being a baffled foreigner. He carries an English phrasebook with him most of the time, and he's generally struggling to get out even one complete sentence without saying something wrong. No matter what anyone does or says to him, his usual response is "Thank you very much." He even says "Thank you very much" to some of Louie's insults. Latka has a habit of mentioning totally inappropriate things in any situation. He'll meet a girl and immediately ask her, "Bed?"

His understanding of the American way of doing things is sketchy at best. For example, he rents a luxurious apartment costing three thousand dollars a month without realizing he can't afford to pay more than one month's rent. At one point Latka is in serious danger of being deported until the gang finds a woman to marry him (in "Paper Marriage"). The woman is a prostitute who only agrees to the marriage because she's being paid for her time at the wedding, but Latka appears disappointed that they aren't going off on a honeymoon. "Boy, America is a tough town," he tells the cabbies after the ceremony.

Several late episodes of *Taxi* reveal that

Latka develops a case of multiple personalities. Besides being his normal self, if Latka can ever be said to be "normal," he sometimes turns into Vic Ferrari, a slimy egomaniac; Arlo, a cowboy; and Alex, based on Alex Rieger. The real Alex Rieger is not at all thrilled about having a double around the garage, so he talks Latka into going to a shrink. Latka goes to several different psychiatrists before he is finally cured by Dr. Joyce Brothers.

Simka is introduced in the episode "Guess Who's Coming for Brefnish?" in which she begins her romance with Latka. At first, there's a big obstacle: Latka and Simka are from rival factions of their country. Simka is one of the mountain people and Latka is a flatlander, and the two groups are sworn enemies. Latka and Simka eventually work out their differences, however. Their wedding is shown in a fourth-season episode of *Taxi;* the ceremony is in keeping with old-country traditions—the groom wears a gown and the bride is dressed like a man.

While Latka is a gentle and innocuous sort of guy most of the time, Simka's personality is more energetic. She has a wild temper, and when angry she lets loose an uninhibited, high-pitched yell. At other times she can be pleasantly agreeable, and in "The Shloogel Show" she becomes a matchmaker and fixes up Alex, Elaine, Louie, and Tony with dates who turn out to be well chosen to suit them.

Although Andy Kaufman and Carol Kane are talented and much of what Latka and Simka say is entertaining, there is something jarring about the difference between the totally absurd style of humor in the scenes that focus mainly on Latka and Simka and the more realistic style of humor in the scenes that focus on the other main characters. This has a disconcerting effect on the viewer: it's like trying to listen to someone whose voice is constantly shuttling in pitch between a deep bass and a high treble. In the first three seasons of *Taxi,* though, when Latka is used mainly to provide brief bits of comic relief, the character works much better than when he later becomes the center of attention of many episodes.

THE SUPPORTING CAST AND THE GUEST STARS

Over the course of five years of episodes, we meet so many distinctive and interesting secondary characters that viewers, like readers of a good novel, come to feel that a world full of real people exists on *Taxi*.

One of the most memorable characters is Alex's ex-wife Phyllis (played by Louise Lasser). Phyllis is highly neurotic: when she prays, she says, "Lord, please bring back two-prescription refills of Valium." And when she comes into a restaurant, she may ask, "Where are lonely, desperate women usually seated?" Alex once describes her by saying that "she lives for confrontations."

Phyllis is very critical of Alex's lack of ambition. Meeting him (in "Fathers of the Bride") for the first time since their divorce, she says, "Eighteen years, and at last. . . . There's so much to talk about. Your life has changed dramatically since I knew you. I hear they have those electronic meters now." Following their divorce, Phyllis moved with their daughter, Cathy, to Brazil, where Phyllis married her second husband, a wealthy gentleman named Carlo Consuelos, whom we meet briefly in "Fathers of the Bride." After her second marriage ends in divorce, Phyllis comes back to America and apparently wants to get back together with Alex, though he doesn't seem enthusiastic about the idea.

Part of Phyllis's appeal on *Taxi* is that she brings out an especially lively side of Alex. He is often glum, and he seems tired in many episodes, but when Phyllis is on the scene, Alex is much more energetic than usual. We can clearly see that their marriage must have been full of all kinds of stormy weather.

And then there's John Burns (portrayed by Randall Carver), who appears as a cabbie in many first-season episodes. John is a confused, shy young man. After he gets married (in "The Great Line"), he wonders if he's made a mistake. "I don't want to be married," he tells Alex. "I don't know—it sounds crazy, but in my mind, it's all connected. You get married, you have kids, you grow old, then you die. Somehow, it seems to me, if you didn't get married, you wouldn't die."

The part of Zena Sherman, Louie's girlfriend, was played by Rhea Perlman.

The producers of *Taxi* originally intended for John to continue as one of the regulars on the series, but they later decided the character wasn't working out, and they dropped John from the show late in the first season. Curiously, he wasn't "written out" of the show: no mention is made in any episode about why John is no longer around. He simply disappears after the episode "Memories of Cab 804, Part II." We are given a few hints, though, about what may have happened to him. John is apparently the worst booker in the garage, and Louie threatens to fire him in several episodes. (In "One-Punch Banta," Alex comes to John's rescue and threatens to quit if John is fired.) And John is the one who wrecks

Cab 804, the oldest cab in the fleet. A likely guess, then, is that John must have been fired by Louie. Was it a smart move for the producers to get rid of the John Burns character? Probably—for the reason that John is a bit on the insipid side, and viewers might well have tired of him. In fact, he was the main focus of only two episodes, "The Great Line" and "Money Troubles."

"To my understanding, the characters of John Burns and Tony Banta were too similar," says Randall Carver. "Both Tony and I were playing innocent and naive characters, so you had two actors there playing the same notes. Some of the lines were almost interchangeable. . . . By the sixth or seventh episode, I was already feeling pretty insecure about the longevity of my character. I could see the writing on the wall." Carver has more recently appeared in the Charles Bronson film *Murphy's Law* and in two made-for-TV movies, *Detour to Terror* and *Flag*. He has also been a guest star on a number of television series, including *The Love Boat*.

Louie's girlfriend, Zena Sherman, is in four episodes. She was played by Rhea Perlman, Danny DeVito's wife, who currently appears on NBC's *Cheers*, in the part of Carla Tortelli, a man-hungry barmaid. On *Taxi*, Rhea's character is a mild-mannered girl who refills the candy machine at the garage. Zena goes out with Louie for a while, but she's eventually unable to put up with Louie's bad points. (After all, putting up with Louie's shortcomings would probably try the patience of Mother Teresa.) In "Zena's Honeymoon," she gets married to Tom, a child psychiatrist, and Louie tells her, "You were the best woman I ever had."

Because of Zena we get to see aspects of Louie that we otherwise would never have glimpsed. We learn about how Louie divides women into good girls and bad girls—and that he can scarcely bring himself to go to bed with a "good" girl. We see him at his lowest ebb on those occasions when he's afraid that he's going to lose Zena: there is no limit to the amount of groveling he's willing to do to get her back.

Louie's mother (portrayed by Danny DeVito's mother, Julia DeVito) makes several appearances; she's every bit as tough-minded as Louie is. Louie treats her about as lovingly as he treats the cab drivers. In one episode ("Louie's Moth-er"), he puts her into a nursing home that he's never even gone to look at himself. When Louie and his mother fight, he hides her false teeth. And when his mother is married to a Japanese man (in "Louie's Mom Remarries"), he only very grudgingly agrees to attend the wedding. After seeing these episodes, we may feel that an Inquisition should be started to burn Louie.

Despite how shabbily he treats her (which is shabbily indeed), Louie's mother does bring out some interesting sides to his character. When he puts her into the nursing home, for example, he soon realizes that he misses her. To get her to come back to live with him, he actually has to admit to his mom that he is "a lonely man"—which must be about as hard for him to do as it would be for most of us to admit to being, say, a child molester.

Elaine's kids, Jason and Jennifer, have important roles in several episodes. They seem to be pretty well behaved, though they also seem proficient at manipulating Elaine into giving them what they want. In "Sugar Ray Nardo," for instance, Jason takes advantage of Elaine's worry that her children are losing something by not having a man around the house. Jason convinces his mother to allow him to take boxing lessons by telling her that his dad would have let him box. (Observant viewers of *Taxi* may notice that Jason is portrayed by two different actors: Michael Hershewe plays him in the early episodes and David Mendenhall plays him in the later ones.)

J. Alan Thomas portrays Jeff Bennett, the assistant dispatcher. Though we see him in the background during many episodes, his role was never developed very much. We don't ever really get a sense of what Jeff is like; the writers of the series never clearly defined the character. Jeff's biggest moment comes in the episode "Crime and Punishment," in which Louie tries to talk Jeff into taking the blame for a scheme to defraud the cab company. Jeff refuses, but nearly winds up being sent to prison for Louie's crimes.

Tommy, the bartender at Mario's, is another character whom we often see but seldom hear from. "I did twenty-four shows," says T. J. Castronova, who played Tommy. "The first year they used several different bartenders and waiters, and finally they settled on me for the next four years." Since *Taxi*, Castronova has gone on to become one of the producers of the syndicated TV series *Tales from the Darkside*.

Many well-known actors and actresses, such as Victor Buono, Ted Danson, Ruth Gordon, Tom Hanks, Penny Marshall, Martin Mull, Mandy Patinkin, Tom Selleck, Wallace Shawn, Martin Short, Nina Van Pallandt, Dee Wallace, and Keenan Wynn, were guest stars on *Taxi*. Although appearing in only one or two episodes, quite a few of these people made important contributions to the series.

One of the finest guest stars was Wallace Shawn, who portrayed Elaine's boyfriend Arnie Ross in two of the later episodes. In the episode "Arnie Meets the Kids," Arnie tries frantically to make a favorable impression on Elaine's children; when he runs out of toys to give Jason and Jennifer, he starts handing out money to them. (Naturally Elaine does not approve of this, and she makes the children give Arnie his money back.) Arnie is one of the most unforgettable of the urban neurotics that we meet on *Taxi*. He has a high-pitched, whiney voice, which gets very loud when he becomes upset. Arnie is anxious to the point of desperation about meeting new people. He tells Alex, "You don't know the work it takes to get people to like me. I put out, man." Anyone who doesn't feel at least a little sorry for Arnie must have a heart as hard as Louie's.

In "Going Home," Victor Buono does a superb job as Reverend Jim's father. He's clearly more than a little disappointed to learn what Jim has made of his life. Victor Buono's character says to Jim, "It's disgusting—to throw away the opportunities you've had, the education, the breeding. And you don't really feel ashamed, do you?" Of course, all of this is completely lost on Reverend Jim, who answers, "Nope."

Even though he only appeared in this one episode, Victor Buono's performance added something important to the series. We certainly have him in mind when we watch those other episodes in which Jim's dad is mentioned—especially "Jim's Inheritance," when Mr. Caldwell dies and tries to leave a large part of his estate to Reverend Jim.

CHAPTER 6

JUDD HIRSCH

The producers of *Taxi* certainly knew what they were doing when they cast Judd Hirsch, a performer with a well-deserved reputation in the theater as a serious dramatic actor, in the role of Alex Rieger. Hirsch's acting on *Taxi* is a triumph of understatement: he plays the character straight and never indulges in the camera-hogging tricks of many comedians. His forte is reacting in a funny way to those around him. Hirsch explains that "what I like to see on a stage or a screen is an actor who *thinks*. I decided [early in my career] that when I played, the audience would watch me think."

James Burrows, the director of many *Taxi* episodes, says, "I've never seen an actor so thorough and methodical. Judd dissects a character on his own time and brings it to work reassembled and whole." Very few performers on television have mastered their craft as completely as Hirsch has. He's a solid professional who can be depended upon to be convincing no matter what he's asked to do or say.

In fact, many fans of *Taxi* may not be aware of just how versatile Hirsch is. In his latest Broadway success, *I'm Not Rappaport*, for which he won the Tony Award

for best actor of 1985, Hirsch transforms himself into a feisty, scheming old man who spends most of his time sitting on a bench in Central Park. At no point does Hirsch allow any trace of Alex Rieger to show through. And when Hirsch played Alex Rieger on *Taxi*, he was most definitely not playing himself (though it is easy for TV viewers to confuse the actor with the part—especially after seeing a character like Alex week after week for years, until he seems to become almost a part of the viewer's own family). In contrast with Alex, Judd Hirsch is an ambitious, hard-driven workaholic and an animated conversationalist. Alex Rieger is a pessimist; Judd Hirsch, more of an optimist.

Hirsch is a native New Yorker, born and raised in the Bronx. He is the son of Joseph Sidney Hirsch, an electrician, and his wife Sally. Judd, born on March 15, 1935, has one brother, Rolland, and no sisters. Judd recalls that when he was growing up, "we were very temporary. We moved a lot within the city, thirteen times before I hit second grade. I don't know what it was. I was never able to figure out why we moved so much—it was probably inner-family turmoil of a sort that I was too young to understand. But I never felt permanent." Judd says that his

Judd Hirsch

Judd Hirsch as Sgt. Dominick Delvecchio.

family was often hard up for money. "At the time I always felt I was very lucky not to be brought up in a total slum. Now, looking back, a lot of the places I lived in *could* be called total slums."

Not surprisingly, since he came from a poor family, Judd says he was encouraged to find a job that offered more security than acting. He was a physics major when he attended the City College of New York, and he originally planned to become an engineer. After a few years of college, however, "I realized that although I was very suited to be an engineer or architect or anybody in science or industry, I realized my mind was starv-ing, and I didn't know what I was going to do. I had no idea." Soon, Hirsch remembers, "I began to look around me, to read, to go to plays; and actors fascinated me. Wow! Guys who could, through their work, have some kind of an effect on society. The instant I enrolled in acting school and stepped on a stage to do a scene in front of people, I knew I'd found a home."

After studying at the American Academy of Dramatic Arts and with well-known acting coaches such as Uta Hagen and William Hickey, Hirsch spent many years performing in obscure theaters and summer stock productions. His first big break was in 1966, when he landed the role of the telephone repairman in Neil Simon's *Barefoot in the Park* on Broadway. In the late sixties and early seventies, Hirsch played important roles in several off-Broadway productions, most notably in 1973 as the night manager in Lanford Wilson's *The Hot L Baltimore*.

An executive for Universal Studios saw *The Hot L Baltimore* and suggested that Hirsch be cast in the part of Murray Stone, a crusading public defender, in a made-for-television movie, *The Law*. *The Law*, broadcast by NBC on October 22, 1974, dealt with a sensational murder trial, and it earned rave reviews and high ratings. Hirsch's performance was singled out for praise by many reviewers, including a critic for *Variety*, who wrote that "Hirsch has emerged full-blown as a performer to be reckoned with—gutsy, brainy, and compassionate beneath his brash, streetwise veneer, and utterly convincing in every aspect of the script. He seems to be one of those actors who has already trimmed all the fat off his technique." Hirsch also appeared in another TV version of *The Law:* a miniseries of three episodes that was broadcast in 1975 and that won an Emmy as the outstanding limited series of the year.

After a few more off-Broadway plays (including Jules Feiffer's *Knock, Knock,* for which Hirsch won a Drama Desk Award) and TV movies, Hirsch starred in the CBS series *Delvecchio* during the 1976–77 season. In that series Hirsch played Sgt. Dominick Delvecchio, a tough Los Angeles police detective. But the program was canceled after the first season; Hirsch argues that "hack writers and directors" were responsible for making *Delvecchio* little more than a formula detective show.

Hirsch's first role in a film made for theatrical release was in the 1978 movie *King of the Gypsies.* Written and directed by Frank Pierson, *King of the Gypsies* is concerned with the conflicts among members of a family of gypsies who live in New York City. Unfortunately, the film was a flop at the box office. Hirsch received his first Emmy Award in 1978, as the outstanding leading actor in a single appearance of a series, for his work as a guest star in an episode of the sitcom *Rhoda* entitled "Rhoda Loves Mike."

Throughout the first half of 1978, Hirsch starred in the hit Neil Simon play *Chapter Two.* Simon recalls that when he wrote *Chapter Two* he imagined Hirsch as the leading character, mainly because of Hirsch's ability to convey both tenderness and strength. Simon explains that "Judd Hirsch has a hard surface and a soft center. He's always concealing one with the other." Hirsch says he was especially eager to play in *Chapter Two* since

"it was a part which I didn't think anybody would ask me to play. At that moment in my career, I was in television. I was being asked to play Italians and tough guys and fast-talking people. So the opportunity was a total actor's opportunity."

When James Brooks and Ed. Weinberger first approached Hirsch to appear in *Taxi,* he turned them down. But Brooks and Weinberger kept asking him to reconsider. Brooks says they wanted him for *Taxi* "because Judd was an attractive male in his early forties who's good in both drama and comedy, and that's a category of actor *impossible* to find."

According to Hirsch, "Jim and Ed simply knew what string to pull. 'We want actors in this,' they told me. 'We want to develop a company, the way *Barney Miller* has done.' Well, I've dreamed of working in a resident company, an actors' ensemble. Still, I told my agent to pass the offer by. The show was to be taped on a soundstage. At first, I thought, 'How the hell can you shoot a taxi show in a Hollywood studio?'" But when Hirsch read the script for the pilot episode ("Like Father, Like Daughter"), he changed his mind. "It was more subtle. The scripts were the real star of *Taxi.* They were always solid. You didn't have to worry about the material being good—the way you have to do with most TV shows."

Hirsch continued to appear in plays and movies during the five years he was on *Taxi.* He received a Tony nomination for his work in *Talley's Folly* (1979), a play written specifically for him by Lanford Wilson; he received an Oscar nomination for his interpretation of the psychiatrist in the movie *Ordinary People* (1980), directed by Robert Redford. (By the way, several scenes from *Ordinary People,* in which Hirsch's character tries to help the teenage boy played by Timothy Hutton to overcome his problems, are reminiscent of scenes from *Taxi* in which Alex Rieger tries to help the other cab drivers.)

In both 1981 and 1983 Hirsch was awarded the Emmy for being the outstanding leading actor in a comedy series. He received the 1983 award shortly after *Taxi* had been canceled, and at the Emmy Award ceremonies he publicly criticized NBC executives for their decision. After being handed his Emmy, Hirsch said, "There are people I don't wish to thank at all tonight. . . . They should really put the show back on the air." (Later, he told reporters he had only been joking when he made those remarks.)

Hirsch has been married and divorced twice and has one son, Alex, from the second marriage. Hirsch has a house in the San Fernando Valley in California and an apartment in Greenwich Village in New York City.

He says he is still somewhat uncomfortable with his success and, especially, with being recognized on the street: "I've always taken subways and buses. I like going into shops and buying things. Now I feel I've curtailed that part of my life, and I want it back. . . . But the longer you're on something like *Taxi,* the more easily recognizable you are, no matter what. After three years on *Taxi,* I was wearing floppy hats pulled down, dark glasses, a beard—and I cut the recognizability down to 50 percent. Another year and I could cut out only 25 percent. If I had been on that show any longer, I'd have to have had plastic surgery."

CHAPTER 7

THE OTHER STARS OF TAXI

MARILU HENNER

Marilu Henner credits her family background for much more than just her striking red hair and green eyes. "I'm the third oldest of six children from a fantastic Polish-Greek family," she says. "My father, Joseph, managed auto dealerships, and my mother, Loretta, had a dancing school in the backyard of our home in Chicago. There were always dozens of kids around, taking dancing lessons at all hours. . . . I took dancing lessons at age two and a half, and there was never any doubt after that I'd be a performer."

Marilu explains that when she acts "the basic color of each of my characters is usually one of the women in my family." She says the character of Elaine Nardo was based on her older sister.

While attending the University of Chicago in 1970, she was invited to try out for a local production of the musical *Grease,* and she did so well in the production that two years later she earned a spot

Marilu Henner may be the most underrated performer on *Taxi.*

in the national touring company. (Jeff Conaway and John Travolta were also in the touring company of *Grease*.)

Over the next few years she appeared in several Broadway productions, the movies *Between the Lines* (1977) and *Bloodbrothers* (1978), and the TV pilots for *The Paper Chase* and *Off Campus*. But her first big national exposure was in commercials. "I did twenty-eight commercials," she says. "I was in the Fruit-of-the-Loom ads, where I was an apple, with only my legs sticking out. I did Playtex bra and girdle ads, too. . . . People saw a lot of me, but only bit by bit!"

Marilu's audition for *Taxi* went over so well with the producers that they decided to cast her as Elaine Nardo, even though they had envisioned the character as about ten years older than Marilu was at the time.

Tony Danza says that Elaine Nardo and Marilu Henner have many qualities in common: "Elaine is the one who gives lectures when the guys get too wild, and plans parties, and looks out for everybody. And that's a lot like Marilu—she's an organizer, she takes responsibility, watches out for her co-workers." Incidentally, Danza admits that he had a crush on Marilu when they worked together on *Taxi*, and he says they once went out on a date.

Like Danza, Jeff Conaway is also a friend of Marilu's. Conaway says, "I was on tour with Marilu in *Grease,* and she was kind of one of the boys, very down-to-earth. We had a platonic company—not the usual sort of thing where everybody's jumping into each other's rooms—and Marilu was like an older sister, the kind you can confide in and know she

won't betray your trust. Still is."

Marilu Henner may be the most underrated performer on *Taxi*. She's never won an Emmy, unlike several of the other actors and actresses, although she certainly deserves one. A reason for this lack of recognition may be that many people are skeptical that anyone as beautiful as she is could also be talented. Yet on *Taxi* Marilu does a fine job, especially of conveying Elaine Nardo's anxieties about raising her children in the best way she can. And Marilu Henner clearly shows us Elaine's ambivalent feelings toward men. Another thing about Marilu's acting on *Taxi* is that she is always unassuming about her looks. We never get the feeling, as we do with so many young actresses, that she is convinced she's gorgeous.

DANNY DEVITO

No one can deliver an insult with more venom than Danny DeVito. His performance as the abrasive, insensitive, pint-sized (DeVito is 5'0″ tall) tyrant Louie DePalma is great fun to watch, and it earned him an Emmy in 1981 for being the outstanding supporting actor in a comedy series.

DeVito was born in Neptune, New Jersey, in 1944, and he grew up in Asbury Park, New Jersey (which is also the home town of Bruce Springsteen). After high school, he went to Manhattan to study at the American Academy of Dramatic Arts, where teachers warned him that landing good roles would be difficult for someone of his height. "I was reminded constantly," DeVito recalls, "that it was going to take a strong talent to make people realize there are short tyrants and tall tyrants, short lovers and tall lovers."

DeVito spent years performing in off-Broadway productions. Trivia buffs should take notice that DeVito first worked with Judd Hirsch in a play entitled *Line of Least Existence,* written by Rosalyn Drexler. Hirsch was the star of the show, while DeVito played a dog named Andy.

The man who did the most for DeVito's career was, without a doubt, Michael Douglas, the son of Kirk Douglas; Michael Douglas and DeVito have been buddies ever since a summer stock production in 1966. In 1973, Kirk Douglas cast DeVito in the film *Scalawag,* and in 1975 Michael Douglas cast DeVito as one of the mental patients in *One Flew Over the Cuckoo's Nest.* The simple-minded, perpetually smiling character named Martini that DeVito plays in *One Flew Over the Cuckoo's Nest* is as different from Louie DePalma as can be imagined. Martini is every bit as mild-mannered as Louie is foul-mannered. Ed. Weinberger says, "When you watch him in *Cookoo's Nest* and then in *Taxi,* you see his range. He's made the character [of Louie DePalma] much more than we had in mind." Other Hollywood producers took note of DeVito's work in *Cuckoo's Nest,* and roles in *Car Wash* (1976) and *Goin' South* (1978) followed.

According to to DeVito, he made quite an impression when he auditioned for *Taxi.* He says he walked into the room where the producers were waiting, slammed his script down on a table, and hollered, "First, there's one thing I want

No one can deliver an insult with more venom than Danny DeVito.

to know before we start: Who wrote this crap?" "After a tense pause," DeVito remembers, "they burst out laughing. I knew I had the part."

DeVito is married to Rhea Perlman (by the way, she's 5' 1"), currently one of the stars of *Cheers* on NBC. She made four guest appearances on *Taxi* as Zena, Louie's girlfriend. And it was on a lunch break from a rehearsal of *Taxi* that Danny and Rhea were married after eleven years of living together.

Tony Danza having a good time in front of the camera.

TONY DANZA

Tony Danza actually was a professional middleweight fighter up to and during his first season on *Taxi*. "I still think boxing was where I had the most natural ability," he says. But after his acting career took off, Danza had to retire from boxing since "other fighters were working at it full time, and I wasn't. . . . To this day, though, I remember moments. I never had a great fight or even a great round, but I did have a few great moments— when you'd throw a perfect left-right-left combination, and the crowd would gasp."

While growing up in a tough neigh-borhood in Brooklyn, Danza did his earliest fighting on the streets: "I was never a malicious kid. But I did get into a lot of fights. I used to love to fight. I never wanted to hurt anybody, though. Today, you can't fight in the streets. For-get it. They'll hit you with a bottle, take you out with a knife. Back then, it was just fists. A pure contest. It was the way to establish yourself. You needed a rep. You had to have respect so you didn't get walked on."

Danza's father, a garbage collector, was a strict disciplinarian. "We had a lot of hitting at home," Danza recalls. "But I'm not a bad kid for it. It was good for me."

After high school in Brooklyn, Danza

went to the University of Dubuque, Iowa, on a wrestling scholarship. In Iowa he met and later married another student at the University. They had two children, Gina and Marc. (Marc was given the role on *Taxi* of Tony Banta's adopted son.) Danza and his first wife were divorced after only two years of marriage.

When he returned to Brooklyn with his college degree, Danza at first wanted to work as a cab driver, but his parents disapproved. According to Tony, his mother said, "You crazy? You want to be a cab driver? Spend all that money and time at school, and you want to be a cab driver? Never!"

So Tony became a boxer—first as an amateur, and then as a professional. "At the beginning I didn't even have a robe," he remembers. "I threw a towel around my shoulders. I got forty dollars for my first [pro] fight. I knocked the guy out." Danza's pro record was four wins and three losses at the time he began to act.

Danza was discovered by Stuart Sheslow, an independent producer, at Gleason's Gym on West 30th Street in Manhattan. For his first acting job, Danza made a pilot for an ABC series, *Fast Lane Blues*, and he was flabbergasted to learn that he was to be paid five thousand dollars for just three weeks' work. After that, Tony went to Hollywood to audition for a movie, *The Warriors*. In a studio hallway on the way to pick up his costume for the audition, he met James Brooks. Brooks was looking for someone to play the boxer on *Taxi*, and he asked Danza to read for the part. (Danza recalls that the role originally called for an Irish heavyweight named Phil Ryan. After Danza got the part, the character's name was changed to Phil Banta, and later to Tony Banta.)

Ed. Weinberger comments that "Tony had absolutely no training to speak as an actor. . . . Yet he fleshed out what on paper was a limited, surface character into something more substantial." On *Taxi*, the way Danza moves, his natural athletic grace, seems so right we feel that Tony Banta is someone out of real life that we know and understand. Furthermore, Danza's boxing ability helps to create a feeling of authenticity in the fight sequences.

One of Danza's best assets on *Taxi* is his sweet, engaging smile. He unmistakably conveys a sense of having a good time in front of the cameras. And when an actor can relax on screen the way he does, he makes the audience feel cheerful, too.

Among his other assets are his dark, Italian features and heavy-lidded, sleepy eyes, which have certainly helped to give him a reputation (apparently a well-deserved one) as a ladies' man. Gossip columnists have paired him with many beautiful young women since he became famous for his role on *Taxi*.

Unlike actors such as Judd Hirsch, who feel slightly uncomfortable with their fame, Danza seems to enjoy immensely his status as a celebrity. He tells about a woman sitting next to him on an airplane who was reading an article about him in *People* magazine. "Is that you?" Danza says she asked him. "Yes," he replied. "And so is this," he added, as he showed her another article about himself in *Newsweek*. "I didn't need that plane," he says. "I could have flown back to Los Angeles myself."

Christopher Lloyd has a flair for handling eccentric characters.

CHRISTOPHER LLOYD

The part of Reverend Jim gives Christopher Lloyd a chance to show off his considerable flair for handling an eccentric character. We are treated to a whole gallery of interesting facial expressions, from wide-eyed stares to grimaces to silly smiles, when we watch Lloyd's interpretation of Jim Ignatowski. The way Jim lumbers around when he walks and the way he puts his hand to his forehead when he's trying to concentrate are also nice touches. Lloyd says, "I enjoy doing complicated or peculiar people . . . characters who have a strange kind of twist to them."

Prior to *Taxi,* Lloyd was best known for his work off-Broadway in a number of plays, including the lead in a much-praised version of Peter Handke's *Kaspar.* Lloyd says that a lot of credit for his acting abilities must go to Sanford Meisner, a teacher at the Neighborhood Playhouse in New York. Before working with Meisner, Lloyd says, "I would be good one night, dull the next. Meisner made me aware of how to be consisent in using the best that I have to offer. But I guess nobody can teach you the knack, or whatever it is, that helps you to come to life on stage."

Most viewers first saw Lloyd in the 1975 film *One Flew Over the Cuckoo's Nest,* which starred Jack Nicholson. Lloyd did an expert job of portraying one of the mental patients, a man filled with an intense rage at everything and everyone around him. "Actually, a great deal of that character, Taber, was improvised on the spot—more and more as the director, Milos Forman, came to trust my reactions," says Lloyd. In 1978 he was in another movie with Nicholson and Danny DeVito, *Goin' South;* Lloyd played the part of a lawman who wants to see the Nicholson character hanged.

During the first season of *Taxi,* Lloyd

made a guest appearance as the minister who married Latka to an American girl. The character of Reverend Jim was so favorably received that Lloyd was asked to join the regular cast of the show for the second season. He recalls, "It was difficult fitting into a format that was already established. . . . I was kind of an outsider in a way. I wasn't *made* to feel that—but, I mean, there was a company that had already been acting together. They didn't ostracize me, though, there wasn't any snob thing."

Members of the cast and crew of *Taxi* say that Lloyd was very soft-spoken and reserved when they worked together. "Chris is so shy," says Marilu Henner. "I rarely talk to him, and I've known him for years. When the Emmies were given out, he sort of had an idea he might win, and the idea of having to get up and accept it in front of all those people was painful to him. Well, he won—but he wasn't there. He's a sensitive, beautiful person, but he doesn't talk much." Lloyd won Emmies for being the outstanding supporting actor in a comedy series in 1982 and 1983.

Though he thinks of himself mainly as an actor in the theater, Lloyd says he enjoys making movies, too. "I've primarily been a theater actor all my life, and you're supposed to have a certain loyalty to the stage. Many of the theater actors in TV and the movies here in Hollywood are always crying about how good it would be to get back to the stage. I just keep doing different roles. I would like to return to it someday, but I feel no great compulsion. . . . It's sort of fun to just go with the flow, to see what comes next."

Jeff Conaway

JEFF CONAWAY

"Bobby Wheeler is a lot like me when I was twenty-one," explains Jeff Conaway. He knows just what Bobby Wheeler has been through. "I lived on Fourth Street between Avenues A and B when I was a struggling actor. It was like a jungle there. . . . Unlike Wheeler, I lucked out and got jobs doing commercials, which kept me going. I could never drive a cab, it's too tough."

Before *Taxi*, Conaway had attracted the most attention of his career for his work in the musical *Grease*. He played he lead at a time when John Travolta was still in the chorus. After two and a half years with the theatrical version, Conaway was also in the movie version of *Grease* (1978).

Conaway has been acting since he was ten years old. Both his mother (who was an actress) and he auditioned for parts in the stage version of James Agee's *A Death in the Family*. Conaway's mother was rejected, but the director liked Conaway's Southern accent (which he had learned during summer vacations at his grandparents' home in South Carolina) and hired him for the production, which starred Lillian Gish, Arthur Hill, and Colleen Dewhurst.

When he was fifteen years old, he formed a rock group named "3½," which performed as an opening act for Chuck Berry, Gladys Knight, and other stars. Later, he enrolled in the North Carolina School of the Arts, and then he transferred to N.Y.U. "I left [N.Y.U.] three months before graduation," he remembers. "There were hard feelings because I had the lead in a school production of *The Threepenny Opera*. But I was offered *Grease* on Broadway. Broadway! I couldn't turn it down."

After his success with *Grease*, Conaway made several TV pilots, and he was given small roles in the movies *The Eagle Has Landed* (1976) and *Pete's Dragon* (1977).

"I was under contract with Paramount when I first heard about *Taxi*," he says.

"Originally I read for the part that Randall Carver wound up playing. Anyway, when I first came to the audition, I was kept waiting and waiting and waiting, and finally Jim Brooks stuck his head out of the door and said, 'Jeff, this is probably the first audition you've ever waited for, because we're just writing the script now.'" A few months later Conaway auditioned again (by that point, the pilot episode had been written), this time for the part of Bobby Wheeler. And the producers made him audition several times more over a period of weeks before he was finally hired. (At one point, they said they were specifically looking for black actors to play Bobby, and Cleavon Little was one of those who auditioned for the role.) "I was both the first and the last actor who read for a part on *Taxi*," Conaway says.

From the first, he realized that his role on *Taxi* was a great opportunity. "The part was a dream for me," he says. "And *Taxi* was an ensemble company, and that's what makes it work." Conaway says that the cast "was so good we could have taken that group of people and put them in any situation, and it would have been funny. We could all have been waiters."

When *Taxi* made him famous, Conaway got a chance to go back to playing rock 'n' roll. He made a record for Columbia in 1979, entitled *Jeff Conaway*, that included some of his own songs. Conaway describes his music as "a cross between Led Zeppelin and Barry Manilow."(!)

After *Taxi* had been on the air for a few seasons, Conaway says he began to feel dissatisfied in some ways with continuing to play Bobby Wheeler. "The reason I left

Taxi," he explains, "was because the role didn't seem to be going anywhere new. I felt I just had to take some chances in my career. I know I missed being on the show, though. I felt a little melancholy for a while afterwards. Looking back on it, it's so difficult to say if it was a mistake to leave the show."

Conaway remembers arguing with the producers about his character. "After three years, I wanted to do things differently, but the character was already cemented. I wanted them to show Bobby as more of a person. Not to show him as a stereotype, always looking at himself in the mirror and thinking of himself as God's gift to women. I wanted to change the concept that people have about ac-

tors. People think that actors are all self-centered and conceited. And week by week there was a lot of that on the show. But when an episode centered on me, I got to say more of what it is really like to be an actor, why we do the things we do. I would've liked to have gotten into it further, but that might have been too serious. You have to remember that it is all supposed to be a comedy."

ANDY KAUFMAN

Andy Kaufman's portrayal of Latka Gravas is based mainly on a character whom Kaufman invented and whom he called the "Foreign Man." Kaufman was

Andy Kaufman

playing the part of this "Foreign Man" character in his stand-up routine at the Comedy Store in Hollywood one night in early 1978 when some of the producers of *Taxi* were in attendance. Soon afterwards, they offered him a part on the series. James Brooks calls Kaufman "a bona fide genius . . . Latka is just one aspect of what he does."

Brought up in a middle-class family in Great Neck, New York, Kaufman put on comedy shows at neighborhood birthday parties when he was still in grade school. While he was attending Grahm Junior College in Boston, he was already working as a comic at the Improvisation night club in New York. By 1978 Kaufman had built up an enthusiastic cult following for his night club act at Catch a Rising Star, the Improvisation, and the Comedy Store. He made fourteen guest appearances on NBC's *Saturday Night Live*—until viewers were given a chance to call in their votes on the question of whether or not he should be kept off the air. Kaufman lost by over thirty thousand votes, and he never appeared again on *Saturday Night Live*.

Andy Kaufman must have been just about the only comedian who could take pleasure in earning the disapproval of a mass audience. Kaufman's style of humor was calculated to take unusual risks, to push himself to the brink of bombing. He would go out of his way to outrage his audiences and provoke them to a strong reaction. For instance, when he portrayed the "Foreign Man" in his stand-up act, he would sometimes talk for ten or fifteen minutes in the "Foreign Man's" incomprehensible language. On other occasions, if an audience failed to laugh at a particular joke, he would repeat it—sometimes over and over again.

In his column for the *Los Angeles Weekly*, Harlan Ellison wrote that Kaufman "was our most valuable comedian because, like Lenny Bruce, he was our most adventurous, our most dangerous funnyman. He expended more courage, took more chances, developed more unsettling, original forms of presentation of his material—which dealt exclusively with aspects of the human condition we'd rather not acknowledge—than anyone working in the medium of stand-up humor."

David Letterman recalls that "we had him on the show [NBC's *Late Night with David Letterman*] as often as we could get him, because I think it's important to have guests who annoy the public. It feels good to scream at the TV once in a while, to go to work the next day and tell everyone how annoyed you are. Andy was a real showman. And he was unique. . . . He was one of my favorite guests."

"I push myself with new material," Kaufman told an interviewer for *TV Guide*, "and create new forms of strangeness that can't work in a mass TV format. Like once in Iowa, I started reading *The Great Gatsby* aloud, to see how far people'd go with it. When I finished at four in the morning, people were still listening. Once when I did the Improv West in Hollywood, I took a portable dryer on stage and did my laundry. People simply wouldn't believe it."

In 1979 Kaufman's Carnegie Hall performance made news when he invited all 2,800 members of the audience out for a late-night snack after the show. Those who attended were driven by bus to the

Manhattan School of Printing, where, courtesy of Andy Kaufman, they were served 2,800 pints of milk and thousands of chocolate-chip cookies.

The "Foreign Man" was Kaufman's most famous character, but in his comedy routines Kaufman was noted for dazzling audiences with a series of different impersonations, each seemingly more outrageous than the last. Kaufman could change from the "Foreign Man" to an excellent impression of Elvis Presley to an "intergender world wrestling champion." Kaufman's own favorite character was Tony Clifton, a slick (and obnoxious) Las Vegas saloon singer who was the model for the Vic Ferrari character on *Taxi*.

Excepting Kaufman, the other members of the cast of *Taxi* have all said they are fans of the series. Tony Danza, for one, says he often watched the syndicated reruns of *Taxi* on Channel 5 in New York. But Kaufman said he thought the show was unadventurous. "As for *Taxi*," he told *TV Guide*, "it's a vehicle, just that. I only tape one-and-a-half days a week, and my contract specifies a limited number of appearances per season."

Carol Kane

CAROL KANE

When she made her first episode of *Taxi* in 1979, Carol Kane was already a veteran of twenty-three films (including *Carnal Knowledge*, *The Last Detail*, *Dog Day Afternoon*, and *Annie Hall*), even though she was only twenty-six years old. As a matter of fact, Carol has been acting ever since she was eight; her first role was in a production of *The Wizard of Oz* at a theater in Cleveland, her birthplace.

When she was sixteen she toured with the road company version of *The Prime of Miss Jean Brodie*. "I have never wanted to be anything but an actress. . . . I'll do anything to be around a theater. If I'm not working at it, I always get depressed." Apparently, Carol is a workaholic with a vengeance. "Work is the most nourishing thing so far in my life. I have fun at work. I make my relationships at work. I get myself out of bed to go to work."

Carol Kane's unusual looks have been one of her best professional assets. She's beautiful in an uncommon, intriguing way, more like a silent movie star than an actress of the eighties. Her delicate features and forlorn eyes may remind viewers of the sort of women shown in many paintings by Botticelli. "I have a hard time giving up the look I like," she explains. "I think maybe in the 1930s and '40s it was more acceptable to be an eccentric type as an actress. Now it's the cover-girl look."

Early in her career she concentrated on plays and movies, but by 1979 she was also considering roles for television. James Brooks recalls, "Carol came to see me for advice on doing TV. She did a guest spot on *Taxi*, to see how she would do. It went through the roof. She did two more spots and won an Emmy for her second appearance. I think she respected our show, respected the actors. And she brought a wonderful spirit to the company."

As soon as she became a regular member of the cast, Carol got Andy Kaufman to teach her the language he invented for Latka. She says she made her first attempt to master the language when Kaufman invited her to dinner and then refused to speak any more English for the rest of the evening. "Andy got a very specific sound to it," Carol recalls. "The script was in English. You just open your mouth and dive in."

Carol says she loved playing Simka, particularly since the character is so different from her own personality. "I get a kick out of her. . . . Whatever comes into her brain, she spits out. I'm not like that, and when I am, I tend to regret it. I mull a lot over what I do. There's a whole lot of stuff I feel free to express in Simka's voice that I cannot express in my own voice. She is liberating. She is direct."

And Carol says that making *Taxi* was a good experience for her because "I learned a lot on *Taxi* about controlling my temper. It is clear to me that [the members of the cast] made a great deal of effort in being decent to each other. That made for an indescribable warmth."

THE PEOPLE BEHIND THE CAMERA

axi was able to maintain a high level of quality throughout most of the 114 episodes mainly because of the work of a large number of people we never see on camera: the producers, directors, writers, set designers, and many others. Quite a few of those people (including the executive producers, James Brooks, David Davis, Stan Daniels, and Ed. Weinberger) were veterans of *The Mary Tyler Moore Show.*

Of all the producers, writers, and directors who worked on *Taxi,* the most influential was James Brooks. (He is listed in the credits not only as one of the creators and executive producers of the series, but also as the "executive creative consultant.") "Jim Brooks was the one who would come up with an answer when nobody else could," recalls Jeff Conaway. Brooks was involved in some way with almost all the episodes of *Taxi,* and he thought up dozens of story ideas—even though he receives credit on the screen for writing only one episode, "Like Father, Like Daughter." Typically, Brooks

or one of the other producers would come up with a basic story idea for each episode in a "pitch session" involving the top producers and writers. Then one writer would be assigned to actually produce a script, usually about thirty pages long.

Ian Praiser, one of the producers of *Taxi.*
(Courtesy of Stephen J. Cannell Productions)

Brooks and the other producers would also be involved in the process of rewriting the scripts, which would continue right up until the day of filming before an audience.

Regular viewers of *Taxi*, whether they are aware of it or not, are familiar with Brooks's laugh. If the viewer listens carefully to a rerun of any *Taxi* episode (or any *Mary Tyler Moore* episode), there's no mistaking a certain "honking" sound, sort of like the sound of a goose, that Brooks makes when he laughs. "It's in every show," says Weinberger. "It's like a signature. It's unique because he's not laughing with everybody else. He hears things that other people don't hear."

Before *Taxi*, Brooks was best known as one of the creators of *The Mary Tyler Moore Show*. He has also created such programs as *Room 222*, *Rhoda*, and *Lou Grant*. His first involvement in television was not with a sitcom, though, but as a reporter with CBS News. "I still, today, have warm thoughts about getting back into news," says Brooks. "There was no caste system, no bureaucracy, in the CBS newsroom. Everybody shared their feelings with everybody else. Edward R. Murrow, Eric Sevareid, Fred Friendly, Hughes Rudd—they were emotional people with great integrity."

A number of people who were involved in making *Taxi* say that Brooks has one of the best story minds in television. But like many other creative people, Brooks has his share of eccentricities, too. Ian Praiser, one of the producers of *Taxi*, explains that "Jim's mind is going a thousand different directions at once. You don't know where he is at any particular moment. Sometimes you want to say, 'Jim, would you like to come down to earth and tell us what you're thinking?' And sometimes he would look right at you, but his mind would be a thousand miles away. And then after a long pause, he'd suddenly dictate a scene off the top of his head, and it would be wonderful."

All of Brooks's shows share an important quality: they're all based on characters from real life. The comedy depends on the audience recognizing the situations as ones we've all been through. "Character is what fascinates me," explains Brooks. "I love populated things."

The other three executive producers of *Taxi*—Stan Daniels, David Davis, and Ed. Weinberger—also played decisive roles in developing the series. Prior to *Taxi*, Daniels, Davis, and Weinberger had been writers and producers for Mary Tyler Moore Enterprises, working not only on *The Mary Tyler Moore Show* (produced by Weinberger), but also on *The Bob Newhart Show* (produced by Davis), *Rhoda*, and others. David Davis is a few years older than the others (Davis directed episodes of *Dobie Gillis* in the early sixties); he retired from his executive producer's job on *Taxi* after the first season. "Stan Daniels was the quietest of the four of them," says Ian Praiser, "but when he spoke it was taken very seriously." One thing about Ed. Weinberger that viewers of *Taxi* may have noticed is that he spells his first name with a period at the end. "Please allow me my affectation," Weinberger says. And the credits for *Taxi* always list him as Ed. Weinberger.

"The creativity of the executive producers was awesome," remembers Praiser. "It was an experience to be in a room with the group of them."

Jeff Conaway says, "Those guys just knew what was funny and what wasn't. I learned a lot from working with them."

"Because of those people, there was an atmosphere on *Taxi* in which you weren't afraid to make unusual suggestions," explains Katherine Green, the executive story editor for the last season of the show. "There was lots of give-and-take. It was a unique series in that the producers weren't afraid to do inventive things. That's why there was stuff on *Taxi* you wouldn't get in other series."

Viewers of *Taxi* may be puzzled (and with good reason) about the wealth of titles listed in the credits at the end of each episode. Especially in the later seasons, the proliferation of titles seemed to be getting out of hand. We see people listed as producers, associate producers, executive producers, story editors, story consultants, executive script consultants, program consultants, executive consultants, and several other titles. To some extent, the titles served to designate a division of labor or to note that one person was subordinate to another. But in some ways the titles had little meaning—often what happened on an episode was that a group of people sat around a table and exchanged ideas on a fairly equal footing with one another.

The people listed at the beginning of each episode as simply the "producers" may have been the most overworked members of the staff of *Taxi*. They were the people most involved in overseeing the day-to-day operations of making an episode of the show. (From all accounts, the job of producer is especially designed for someone who's curious about what it would be like to have nervous break-downs on a regular basis.) For the first three seasons of *Taxi*, the Charles brothers, Glen and Les, were in this position. Glen and Les Charles were also veterans of Mary Tyler Moore Enterprises; in fact, the first script they sold as a comedy-writing team was to *The Mary Tyler Moore Show*. They also wrote for *Phyllis* and *The Bob Newhart Show*.

Ian Praiser, a producer of *Taxi* during the fourth season, describes the routine that was followed during the weeks that *Taxi* was in production: "On Monday we would sit around a table and read the script for the first time. Based on that first reading, we would go back and start rewriting, while the actors would go onto the stage and start their work. Sometimes most of the script would be thrown out at this point. (And before it even got to the table on Monday, it had already gone through an amazing amount of work, sometimes many drafts.) After the Monday reading, the actors rehearsed, so that on Tuesday we could see the script 'on its feet,' so to speak. The director would have the actors ready to show it to us at the end of the day on Tuesday, and then we would see just how much trouble we were in. Based on Tuesday's reading, we would do a rewrite on Tuesday night that could extend into the wee hours of the morning. On Wednesday the actors got a new script, and we continued the rewrite process based on the run-through we saw that day. On Thursday the cameras came in, and the director blocked the cameras to the action. And Friday was when the show came before a live audience—still with rewrites happening, because there were run-throughs every day. It's all like a very shortened version of doing an off-

Broadway show. On TV, though, it's very truncated, very intense. That's why it's a miracle that the quality can be good, because it's like doing twenty-four one-act plays a year. . . . And a good *Taxi*, I think, can stand up against a one-act play from off-Broadway."

The members of the cast and crew explain that what we see on *Taxi* is the result of a great deal of nonegocentric collaboration. The producers, writers, directors, and actors all exchanged ideas during the four days of rehearsals before each episode was filmed (though the executive producers had the final say on important matters). Sometimes the actors wrote the lines that their characters spoke. As Judd Hirsch remembers, "Almost from the first day, we developed a feeling of an ensemble company, a family where we could give and take suggestions easily."

Another important *Mary Tyler Moore Show* alumnus was James Burrows, the director of seventy-six episodes of *Taxi*. He won Emmies in 1980 and 1981 for outstanding directing in a comedy series. Burrows is credited with being one of the first directors of a TV series to use four cameras simultaneously. (In the sixties and early seventies most sitcoms used three cameras.) "With our four-camera technique on *Taxi*," Burows explains, "there weren't many interruptions. . . . And it was like doing a play. We rarely had to reshoot things."

Burrows also had the job on *Taxi* of casting many of the small guest roles. He says, "I'm frankly not very fond of casting, because I think it makes people uncomfortable, including me. But it's something I spent a lot of time and en-

ergy on. . . . When I cast, I try to look for actors who are good and who look interesting. I don't want my choice to be right on the nose, not the obvious. . . . If you cast a type, you limit yourself."

Michael Zinberg, who had been the executive producer of *The Bob Newhart Show*, directed six episodes of *Taxi* during the last two seasons. He explains that "they had had some problems in the fourth year finding directors who would satisfy the cast and the producers, and live up to the standards set by Jim Burrows." (Burrows directed nearly all the episodes of the show during the first three seasons, but he directed only occasionally later on.) Zinberg says, "The actors told me, 'It was nice to work with you because we haven't been able to find someone who was able to communicate with us. . . .' The cast of *Taxi* had somewhat of a repu-

Michael Zinberg, one of the directors of the series

tation for being difficult—which I never found at all. I found them to be the most cooperative, inventive, interesting group of people, a hell of a cast. And easy to work with."

Besides the excellence of the cast, Zinberg remembers the four-camera technique as another thing that made *Taxi* different from other series. "Other shows had used four cameras on special occasions," he says, "but *Taxi* was the first show to use four cameras all the time. This was because of the large number of people in the cast. You wanted to record all of those performances and get them all right the first time. The size of the set was another reason for using more cameras: it was the biggest set that had been used in a sitcom up until that time."

The position of story editor (or script consultant) was an important one, and several people held that job on *Taxi* during the course of the five seasons of the show. Subordinate to the producer, the story editor was responsible for developing scripts. Ian Praiser, who was a story editor during the second season, explains that "story editors write as many episodes as they can get into their contract. And they're part of the rewrite sessions on most of the episodes that year." Praiser recalls, "You start out the season several scripts ahead, but by the middle of the season you're flying by the seat of your pants, just scrambling to meet the schedule."

Barry Kemp, the executive script consultant for the second and third seasons, explains, "We would begin preproduction in April or May at the beginning of the season, even though we didn't begin shooting until July. So we would usually

have about seven or eight scripts ready in July when the shooting started. By the end of the season, though, it was always crazy time."

David Lloyd was another story editor of *Taxi* and another veteran of *The Mary Tyler Moore Show*. (He wrote the Emmy Award-winning "Chuckles Bites the Dust" script for *Mary Tyler Moore*.) He was also the author of several of the best episodes of *Taxi*, including "Jim Gets a Pet," "Elaine's Strange Triangle," "Louie Bumps into an Old Lady," "Jim Joins the Network," "Nina Loves Alex," "Alex the Gofer," and "Louie Moves Uptown."

"Scripts are always massively rewritten," explains Lloyd. "Nothing ever comes out the way you originally write it, even by the best writers. It's a queston of writing and retooling with the cast day after day."

Another *Taxi* story editor (during the third season) was Ken Estin, who was also responsible for writing an impressive number of the best scripts of the series. "What Price Bobby?" "Alex Jumps Out of an Airplane," "Fledgling," "Vienna Waits," "Tony's Lady," "The Shloogel Show," and "Jim's Inheritance"—all excellent episodes—were written by Estin.

Other writers who were responsible for some of the better episodes of *Taxi* were Glen Charles, Les Charles, Howard Gewirtz, Katherine Green, Daniel Kallis, Barry Kemp, Michael Leeson, Earl Pomerantz, Ian Praiser, and Sam Simon.

The executive story editor for the fifth season was Katherine Green. She explains that "the better writers realize they have to do lots of rewriting when it comes to the later drafts, after the actors have

Barry Kemp wrote fourteen episodes of *Taxi.*

read it." She also remembers, "Sometimes new lines were being written minutes before we filmed the show."

Barry Kemp says that "sometimes we would even rewrite right in front of the audience. We'd stop things and redo a sequence with a different punchline."

And Kemp recalls one occasion (during the making of "Bobby and the Critic") when he was nearly forced to do some major rewriting on a Friday evening, with the audience present. "At seven-thirty on Friday," says Kemp, "Stan Daniels came up to me and said, 'We can't find Andy Kaufman. And if we don't find him in five minutes, we'll have to write him out of the show.' At that point it was panic time. The whole audience was already there. So how could we have written him out of the show at that point? I remember we held things up for

fifteen minutes while they looked everywhere for him. Finally, they found him in the parking lot. He had gone off to meditate—he did transcendental meditaton—and had crawled into a car and fallen asleep."

Many of the sets that we see most often on *Taxi,* including the basic Sunshine Garage set and the set for Mario's, were the work of Tom John, the art director for the first season. John also devised the set that was used in filming the scenes that took place inside of cabs. Those scenes were performed on the same stage as all of the other scenes from *Taxi;* the front end of a cab was sawed off so that the audience could see what was happening inside. That's why it is always night during the scenes in the cabs on *Taxi*—there would have been no way to depict realistically the view that would have been visible out of the back windows of the cabs during the daytime. The producers felt that the traditional back-projection method, used in most Hollywood movies from the thirties and forties, would have looked transparently phony on a realistic show like *Taxi.*

Kemp recalls that "in those scenes showing the interiors of cabs, they had an interesting little panel that was set up behind the cab: a black panel with tiny lights that moved and appeared to the camera as if they were headlights. On the panel, though, if you looked at them closely on the stage, they didn't look like car lights at all. And they also had lights on the side of the cab that they would occasionally spin, which would give the illusion of a car passing by or turning."

"The boxing sequences were also done on the stage," adds Kemp, "with a very elaborate ring setup. And lots of smoke, too. They were beautifully done."

Ian Praiser says that "the stage was big enough to hold three sets, side by side. For instance, the set of the garage might be next to the set of Mario's—so all the cameras had to do was to move over. We wouldn't have to completely change the sets between scenes, though we might have to do some redressing or move a wall in during the break."

On those nights when *Taxi* was filmed, Kemp remembers that "at seven-thirty one person—and at one point that job fell

For the scenes inside of cabs, the art director used a black panel with lights "that moved and appeared to the camera as if they were headlights."

to me—would go out and do the warm-up for the audience. I'd say 'hi' and introduce the cast and talk between scene breaks, answer questions and in general help keep things moving. Sometimes it was sort of like a stand-up comedy routine. . . . And then at the end of the night there were invariably one or two hours' worth of pick-ups after the audience had left." (Pick-ups are short retakes of shots that hadn't turned out quite right during the original filming.)

Regular *Taxi* watchers will surely have noticed that we see a great variety of different shots of cabs on the streets of New York. Many of those exterior shots were simply taken from libraries of stock footage: after all, Manhattan street scenes involving cabs have appeared in lots of movies and TV shows. But some of the exteriors were shot specifically for *Taxi*. "The second unit would be sent to New York before the start of every season to get some shots of cabs pulling in and out of the garage," explains Kemp. The location used on *Taxi* for the Sunshine Cab Company was the Dover Garage, located at the corner of Hudson and Charles Streets in Greenwich Village in Manhattan. Those fans who make a trip to the Dover Garage will discover that the place looks almost exactly the same as it did when the series was filmed—and that the cab drivers there are tired of hearing about *Taxi*.

One other person who made an important contribution to the series must be mentioned: Bob James, who was responsible for most of the music heard on *Taxi*. James is well known in the jazz world, with a number of record albums and movie scores to his credit. He also performs occasionally in night clubs. "With the success of *Taxi*, on reruns," says James, "I've been told that twenty-four hours a day, seven days a week, my theme song is playing somewhere in the world, and I'm very pleased about that."

The Sunshine Garage is actually the Dover Garage, located in New York City.

CHAPTER 9

TRIVIA QUIZ

Questions:

1. *How did Reverend Jim get into Harvard?*
2. *What is Simka's maiden name?*
3. *Which members of the regular cast won Emmies for their performances on* Taxi?
4. *What's Louie's favorite TV program?*
5. *Who played Jeff Bennett, the assistant dispatcher?*
6. *What's Reverend Jim's favorite rock group?*
7. *In which cab did a young woman (played by actress Regi Baff) have a baby?*
8. *Bobby appeared in television commercials for three different products. What kinds of products was he promoting?*
9. *What is Jim Ignatowski's real last name?*
10. *Which member of the cast of* Taxi *directed several episodes?*
11. *Which one of the creators of* Taxi *appeared in an episode?*
12. *Who screams in his sleep?*
13. *Who owns a set of Time-Life books on* The Great Lizards?
14. *What was the name of the dispatcher for the Sunshine Cab Company before Louie got the job?*

15. *What does "nik-nik" mean in Latka's language?*
16. *What is Reverend Jim's favorite sitcom?*
17. *Who said, "I like to think a man is never too old to be a flunky"?*
18. *What's the first name of Tony's father?*

Sometimes it seems as if Alex and Louie aren't even speaking the same language.

A scene at the Sunshine Garage from a first-season episode

19. *What were the last names of the two different owners of the Sunshine Cab Company?*

20. *How much does Louie charge to take a phone message?*

21. *Which cab driver was the worst booker in the garage?*

22. *Who once worked as an upholsterer?*

23. *For how many years was Louie a cab driver?*

24. *Who doesn't like having anyone touch his hair?*

25. *How many times did Elaine and Alex sleep together?*

26. *What is Mr. Ratledge's first name?*

27. *Who said, "One thing about being a cabbie is that you don't have to worry about being fired from a good job"?*

28. *Where did Jim's horse (named Gary) die?*

29. *What was Gary's "slave name"?*

30. *Which cabbies held the position of shop steward?*

31. *Who owns the Sunset Nursing Home?*

32. *What is the most popular TV series in Latka's country?*

33. *Which cabbie is a fan of Stephen Sondheim?*

34. *What borough is Reverend Jim's apartment located in?*

35. *Who did Tony accuse of having a dry sense of humor?*

36. *Who said, "When I think of me, I smile"?*

37. *Who temporarily replaced Latka as the mechanic for the garage?*

38. *What is Elaine's maiden name?*
39. *What experience did Tony Banta have as an actor?*
40. *How many fights did Tony Banta lose by knockout?*
41. *What's the name of the gallery where Elaine works?*
42. *What did Mr. MacKenzie do when the Sunshine Cab Company went bankrupt?*
43. *Who said, "Whenever I hear the word 'marriage,' I say, 'Check, please'"?*
44. *What is Louie's mother's first name?*
45. *What was the name of the TV pilot that Bobby was in?*
46. *What's the name of Bobby's agent?*
47. *Bobby grew up in which borough?*
48. *What is Phyllis's maiden name?*
49. *How many times did Reverend Jim go to see E.T.?*
50. *Who was the narrator of "As the Loser Turns"?*
51. *Who took violin lessons as a child?*
52. *Who played soccer in high school?*
53. *Who is the day bartender at Mario's?*
54. *What's the first name of Elaine's ex-husband?*
55. *How much did Jim's father weigh?*
56. *What were the names of Tony's goldfish?*
57. *Who once picked up Errol Flynn in his cab?*
58. *What is Alex's stepbrother's name?*
59. *Who sings "Ebb Tide" in one episode?*
60. *Who are Jim's four heroes?*

Answers:

1. *His father financed a gymnasium for the school.*
2. *Dahblitz*
3. *Judd Hirsch, Danny DeVito, Carol Kane, and Christopher Lloyd*
4. The Phil Donahue Show
5. *J. Alan Thomas*
6. *The Kinks*
7. *Cab 804*
8. *Beer, athlete's foot spray, and suntan lotion*
9. *Caldwell*
10. *Danny DeVito (He directed three episodes.)*
11. *Ed. Weinberger (He appeared in "The Ten Percent Solution.")*
12. *Reverend Jim*
13. *Louie*
14. *Tom*
15. *Making love*
16. The Bob Newhart Show
17. *Alex*
18. *Angelo*
19. *MacKenzie and Ratledge*
20. *One dollar*
21. *John Burns*
22. *Alex*
23. *Fifteen years*
24. *Bobby*
25. *Once*
26. *Ben*
27. *Alex*
28. *In bed*
29. *On Dasher*
30. *Elaine and Tony*
31. *Louie*
32. The Honeymooners
33. *Alex*
34. *Brooklyn*
35. *Alex*
36. *Reverend Jim*
37. *Jeff*
38. *Elaine O'Connor*
39. *He appeared in a grade school production of* Rip Van Winkle.
40. *Fourteen*
41. *The Hazeltine Gallery*

42. *He shot his accountant.*
43. *Latka (as Vic Ferrari)*
44. *Gabriela*
45. Boise
46. *Sid*
47. *The Bronx*
48. *Phyllis Bornstein*
49. *Sixty-four times*
50. *Louie*
51. *Louie*
52. *Alex*

53. *Dwight*
54 *Vince*
55. *410 pounds*
56. *George and Wanda*
57. *Louie*
58. *Mel*
59. *Alex*
60. *St. Thomas Aquinas, Mahatma Gandhi, Alan Alda, and Louie DePalma*

CHAPTER 10

THE EPISODES

FIRST-SEASON CREDITS

Alex Rieger—Judd Hirsch
Elaine Nardo—Marilu Henner
Louie DePalma—Danny DeVito
Tony Banta—Tony Danza
Bobby Wheeler—Jeff Conaway
Latka Gravas—Andy Kaufman
John Burns—Randall Carver

Executive Producers—James Brooks,
    Stan Daniels, David Davis, and Ed.
    Weinberger
Producers—Glen Charles and Les
    Charles
Associate Producer—Budd Cherry
Executive Consultant—James
    Brooks
Director—James Burrows
Film Editor—M. Pam Blumenthal
Art Director—Tom H. John
Director of Photography—Edward E.
    Nugent
Unit Production Manager—Gregg
    Peters
Music—Bob James

Alex tries to reach his daughter, Cathy, in Brazil in a scene from "Like Father, Like Daughter."

"LIKE FATHER, LIKE DAUGHTER"

Episode #1

Synopsis: A pay telephone goes out of order, and the cabbies are able to place calls anywhere in the world for free. At first Alex says, "I don't have anybody to call," but the other cab drivers convince him to try and reach his seventeen-year-old daughter, Cathy, who lives with his ex-wife in Brazil. Alex learns that Cathy is traveling to Portugal, where she'll be attending college, and that she will be changing planes in Miami the next day. Bobby, John, Tony, and Latka all volunteer to takes turns driving, and they get into a cab with Alex and then race to see if they can make it to Miami in time for Alex to meet Cathy. Alex's talk with his daughter lasts only five minutes, but they seem to hit it off pretty well.

Credits: James Burrows directed the script by James Brooks, Stan Daniels, David Davis, and Ed. Weinberger. Talia Balsam played Alex's daughter, Cathy Consuelos.

Hirsch says he agreed to be in *Taxi* because of the quality of the writing for this episode. "When I read the script, it was *not* a lot of one-liners about crazy New York cabbies, but about lives, the human condition."

A reviewer for *Variety* said that in this episode, "Hirsch is gruffly sentimental and appealing . . . but both the script and direction for this initial show had a hurried feeling about them, as though the producers were afraid that the audience would be bored if the show slowed down." Fans of *Taxi* may have trouble understanding what the *Variety* reviewer was complaining about, for "Like Father, Like Daughter" is quite an amusing episode. And it provides a good introduction to several of the main characters, especially Alex. The meeting of father and daughter seems believable, with Alex not knowing what to say to her and Cathy not knowing how to react to him.

"BLIND DATE"

Episode #2

Synopsis: Alex becomes intrigued by the sexy voice of Angela Matusa, a woman from Bobby's answering service. They have a long conversation one day and Alex considers dating her. He asks Bobby about Angela, but Bobby has never met her and says he'd never go out with somebody unless he knew she was attractive. "Well, I might," Bobby says to Elaine, "if I were really drunk." Alex asks Angela out to dinner, and he goes to her apartment to pick her up—where he discovers she's very fat. Though she was witty and pleasant on the phone, in person Alex finds her to be the surliest, most bitter woman he's ever met. The next day Alex says to Elaine, "All night long she kept accusing me of going through the motions, that I wouldn't call her again because of her looks. And I kept telling her she was wrong . . . but she wasn't wrong." Yet he does go back to see Angela again and explains that he would like them to become friends. "I haven't been romantically involved in eight years,"

Alex meets Angela Matusa in "Blind Date."

and the episode ended as he and his fat friend hugged. Vivacious isn't exactly the word for Hirsch, who looks like a candidate for Glummest Living American, with his air of round-shouldered defeat and a blunt, homely puss that barely supports one facial expression. His delivery is flat as a slab but somehow wonderful, and he gets more out of a morose stare than some comics get out of a whole repertoire of mugging."

Observant fans of *Taxi* will notice that the same actress, Suzanne Kent, returns (minus an amazing number of pounds) in Episode #30, "The Lighter Side of Angela Matusa."

Another note about this episode: "Blind Date" won a Humanitas Prize in 1979 for James Brooks.

says Alex. He tells her he's not looking for romance, just someone he can enjoy talking to. By the end of "Blind Date," Angela finally loosens up and shows that she can be agreeable when she wants to be. We see that Alex and Angela will probably become good friends.

Credits: James Burrows directed the script by Michael Leeson. Suzanne Kent played the part of Angela Matusa.

In his column for *TV Guide*, Robert MacKenzie wrote about this episode, saying that "Hirsch's blind date turned out to be an immensely fat girl who greeted him defensively at the door: 'You wanta come in? You got guts.' The cabbies ragged him mercilessly about his rotund date, but his big, soft heart was touched,

"THE GREAT LINE"

Episode #3

Synopsis: John, Bobby, Tony, Elaine, and Alex are drinking beers at Mario's one day when John becomes interested in a pretty girl sitting across the room. John is shy about approaching her, so Bobby and Tony come up with a "foolproof" line for him to use with her. John walks over to her and says, "Let's cut the preliminaries. You want to get married?" John is given a real surprise when she responds by saying "yes." Of course, the girl, Suzanne Caruthers, is only joking. Yet they soon actually do get married, since neither of them calls the "joke" off. (They drive to Maryland for the cere-

"Let's cut the preliminaries. You want to get married?" John asks Suzanne in "The Great Line."

meet and get married almost immediately, but it was a difficult situation to make believable. I think it worked out well, though, and the audience responded warmly to it. . . . I especially liked John's line about the feeling that if you don't mature, if you don't get married, then you somehow feel as if you wouldn't have to get old and die. I'm forty now and haven't been married, and I can see now that the writers were saying something that is right out of my own personal psyche. . . . I can really identify with what John says."

"COME AS YOU AREN'T"

Episode #4

mony.) They are genuinely attracted to each other, but everything has happened so fast that a few days later they begin to have second thoughts about the marriage. Suzanne sends John a letter saying, "You're too nice a guy to be stuck with an immature nut like me. Naturally, we'll have the marriage annulled." But after talking it over further (at Suzanne's parents' house), they resolve to try to stay married.

Credits: James Burrows directed the script by Earl Pomerantz. Ellen Regan was the guest star, in the role of Suzanne Caruthers—with Dolph Sweet and Sheila Rogers playing Suzanne's parents. Rusdi Lane played the bartender at Mario's, and William Foster was the stranger.

About this episode Randall Carver comments, "It's true that a few people do

Synopsis: Elaine throws a cocktail party to impress her art-world acquaintances and asks Alex to accompany her. The other cabbies overhear the plans for the party and invite themselves (Louie remarks, "Perhaps some of those art-world cuties might want me to pose for them *au naturel*"), much to the worry of Elaine. She is not only concerned about how Bobby, Tony, John, and Latka may act (she refuses to allow Louie to attend), but she's afraid that her snobbish guests will learn she is a cab driver. At the party, though, it turns out to be Elaine who slips up and reveals she's a cabbie. However, most of her art-world friends actually admire her diligence in holding down two jobs.

Credits: James Burrows directed the script by Glen Charles and Les Charles. Andra Akers was Rita, Paula Victor was

Tony Banta spars with Carlos Navarone in "One-Punch Banta."

Mrs. Hazeltine, William Bogert was Broderick, and Clyde Kusatsu was Paul. All of these characters were guests at Elaine's party.

Because Alex and Elaine are people the viewer has come to care about, the conflicts between them are especially memorable. In this episode Elaine has a lot of trouble convincing Alex to lie about what he does for a living. After he agrees—very reluctantly—to cooperate with her scheme, we're treated to a wonderful display of Judd Hirsch's skills as a comic performer as Alex ad-libs a ludicrous story about being an oil-well firefighter. "All holocausts may look alike," Alex tells a woman from the art gallery, "but each one has a personality all its own."

"ONE-PUNCH BANTA"

Episode #5

Synopsis: Tony gets a chance to be the sparring partner for a world-champion boxer, Carlos Navarone. The other cabbies chip in and buy Tony his first boxing robe, and they all come to the gym to watch him spar with the champ. To everyone's amazement, Tony apparently lands a solid punch and knocks Navarone down. Because of his surprisingly good showing with the champ, Tony gets a fight against Frankie Wallace, a major contender, at Madison Square Garden. (Tony says, "*Ring* magazine has him rated eighth in the world. I'm not even eighth in the gym.") Before his big fight at the Garden, however, Tony learns that Navarone had taken a dive when he sparred against him, in order to draw more fans to the champ's next fight. Needless to say, Tony is completely outclassed by Wallace in their bout.

Credits: James Burrows directed the script by Earl Pomerantz. Carlos Palomino, the WBC welterweight champion at the time, was the guest star as Carlos Navarone, and Allen Arbus played Jerry Martin.

The producers based the character of Tony Banta very heavily on Tony Danza. For instance, the story that Tony Banta tells in this episode about not having a robe was taken straight from Danza's own experience. And in several episodes, we see that Tony Banta works out at Gleason's Gym, the same place where Tony Danza used to train.

"BOBBY'S ACTING CAREER"

Episode #6

Synopsis: Bobby won't let anybody else use the phone in the garage, because he's expecting to find out if he has landed an important acting part. He tells the other cabbies that when he came to New York he gave himself a deadline of three years to get a professional acting job; if he didn't get one, he would quit. He admits that his deadline will be up in fourteen hours. When the phone call comes through, Bobby learns that he has failed

again. Alex talks him into making one last try, though, and Bobby goes out to audition for anything he is able to find that day. (We see him try out for an E. F. Hutton commercial.) That evening the gang meets at Bobby's apartment, where he awaits a phone call from his agent. A call doesn't come that evening, but Bobby decides to give himself another three years to make it as an actor.

Credits: James Burrows directed the script by Ed. Weinberger and Stan Daniels. John Lehne was Roy Thomas, Jeff Thomas was Jeff, Taurean Bacque was a policeman, Robert Phalen was Tom Jeffries, and Michael Mann was Peter.

"HIGH SCHOOL REUNION"

Episode #7

Synopsis: Louie reveals that he's been invited to his twentieth anniversary high school reunion. He wants to go but feels his job as a taxi dispatcher won't impress his former classmates. Louie admits he was often made fun of in high school for his lack of height. He says he has always dreamed that one day he would avenge himself by going to his class reunion and making everyone there envious of his life. He especially wants a beautiful girl, Sheila Martin, to feel sorry for how she acted toward him. Bobby listens to Louie's story and then suggests that he could go to the reunion and impersonate Louie. Bobby says, "I want a chance to take on this acting job. I may not be getting any other offers. But if I can handle this, I know I'm headed in the right direction." Amazingly enough, Bobby succeeds in fooling Louie's classmates. (He tells them he grew over a foot taller in college.) With his usual charm Bobby makes a highly favorable impression on Sheila Martin. Louie is so curious about how well Bobby is doing that he goes with Alex to the reunion to observe the situation. Luckily, no one seems to recognize the real Louie, and he gets to savor Bobby's triumph.

Credits: James Burrows directed the script by Sy Rosen. Arlene Golonka played Sheila Martin, Joanna Cassidy played Beverly, Pierrino Mascarino played Stanley Tarses, Bob Packard was Mark, Angelo Gnazzo was George, and Sandy Holt was Annette. All of these characters were former classmates of Louie's.

A reviewer for the *Los Angeles Times* wrote that in this episode, "Louie persuaded Bobby to impersonate him . . . because he was too embarrassed to make an appearance himself. Louie's vulnerability has been shown in other ways, too, but he seldom lets his guard down too far. We can usually muster up enough dislike for him by the end of the show because, deep down, he's just not a very likable guy."

"High School Reunion" includes a little inside joke by the *Taxi* writers. The character of Stanley Tarses, the guy who made fun of Louie in high school, is named after Jay Tarses, one of the producers for Mary Tyler Moore Enterprises.

"PAPER MARRIAGE"

Episode #8

Synopsis: Men from the Immigration Department come to the garage in search of Latka, who faces deportation as an illegal alien. But Alex comes up with a scheme: if Latka marries a U.S. citizen, then he can remain in the country. After Elaine declines to marry Latka, Alex finds a hooker, Vivian, who agrees to the marriage—if she's paid for her time. Next, the cabbies need a minister. So they ask Reverend Jim, an ex-hippie who hangs out at Mario's, to help them. (Reverend Jim was ordained a minister of the "Church of the Peaceful" in 1968.) Jim agrees to perform the ceremony, even though he's never done a wedding before. Immediately after the ceremony is over, the bride leaves—and Latka is disappointed that he'll have no honeymoon. "Boy," he says, "America is a tough town."

Credits: James Burrows directed the script by Glen Charles and Les Charles, from a story by Barton Dean. Christopher Lloyd portrayed Reverend Jim, Rita Taggart portrayed Vivian, James Randolph was Richards, an official from the Immigration Department, and Woody Eny was Lawrence.

Christopher Lloyd does a great scalpel job on sixties burnouts in his first appearance on *Taxi.* James Burrows, the director of many episodes, explains that Lloyd had a hand in shaping the character. At first the producers had tried a variety of different types of ministers for the part of

Reverend Jim, without being satisfied with the results. "It wasn't funny until a man came in who had a whole story behind him," says Burrows. Lloyd's story, of course, was of a man who had been through every cause that came along in the sixties—from LSD to political protests to transcendental meditation. What's left by the late seventies, it seems, is a man who is little more than a vestige of his former self.

One other note: M. Pam Blumenthal won an Emmy in 1979, for outstanding film editing in an episode of a series, as a result of her work on "Paper Marriage."

"MONEY TROUBLES"

Episode #9

Synopsis: John and his new bride Suzanne are having trouble making ends meet; her parents even pay the rent on their small apartment. Latka and Alex are invited over to the newlyweds' apartment one evening, where they hear about John and Suzanne's financial problems. When Suzanne's parents decide to stop paying the rent, it means that either John or Suzanne will have to drop out of college. (John wants to be a forest ranger; Suzanne, a nurse.) Alex comes to their aid, offering to lend them some money—and, after some quarreling between the newlyweds, they accept. At the end Alex is a little upset with himself for always being such an easy touch. "Just another day in the life of Alex Rieger, superjerk," he says.

Credits: James Burrows directed the script by Earl Pomerantz. Ellen Regan was the guest star as Suzanne.

"A FULL HOUSE FOR CHRISTMAS"

Episode #10

Synopsis: A few days before Christmas, Louie's brother Nicky arrives in town. Nicky is a big-time gambler from Las Vegas, and he hasn't seen his mother, who lives with Louie, in six years. Louie wants Nicky to take their mother to Las Vegas for a vacation (Louie says she's getting on his nerves), but Nicky laughs at the idea. For revenge against his brother, Louie talks Alex, the best poker player in the garage, into getting into a high-stakes card game with Nicky. Louie bankrolls Alex in the poker game and hopes to win a lot of money from Nicky. (We learn later that the money Louie puts up really belongs to the Sunshine Cab Company.) In the big poker game Nicky loses several thousand dollars. In addition, he's forced (as another part of his losses) to give his mother a three-week vacation in Las Vegas.

Credits: James Burrows directed the script by Barry Kemp. The guest star, playing Nicky, was Richard Foronjy.

In this episode we first hear about Louie's mother. We don't actually see Mrs. DePalma, but we overhear Louie speaking to her on the phone. At one point he yells at her, "Hey, crazy lady, give me a break here."

"SUGAR MAMA"

Episode #11

Synopsis: Dee Wilcox is a lively and wealthy lady in her seventies; she uses some of her money to hire cabs for the evening to escort her about town. When Dee hails Alex one night, she immediately becomes attached to him; they spend evenings at such places as LaGuardia Airport, where they watch the planes land. She shows her appreciation with exorbitant tips and a cashmere jacket. Alex

Alex becomes a paid companion of Dee Wilcox (played by Ruth Gordon) in "Sugar Mama."

soon becomes uncomfortable with the situation of being a paid companion. At a ballroom where Alex is accompanying Dee one night, he strikes up a conversation with a guy named Ramon, who is obviously a gigolo. (Ramon's shirt is, naturally, unbuttoned almost to the waist. So when Ramon says to Alex, "I like your tie," Alex replies, "Thanks. I like your ribs.") When Alex finds out that Ramon considers him to be a fellow gigolo, it's too much for him to take. Alex demands that Dee stop giving him money and gifts. If they see each other again, he tells her, he'll have to be the one who pays for things. "I just hope my stomach can stand the dumps you can afford," Dee responds.

Credits: James Burrows directed the script by Glen Charles and Les Charles. The guest star was Ruth Gordon, portraying Dee Wilcox. Aharon Ipale played Ramon and Herb Vigran played Weldon Manning.

"Sugar Mama" deservedly won an Emmy Award for Ruth Gordon in 1979 for being the outstanding leading actress in a single performance of a comedy series. The *New York Times* reviewed this episode, saying, "With Miss Gordon pulling out all of her outrageous histrionic stops, Mr. Hirsch played skillfully. . . . The combination was as neatly organized as anything to be seen in a current play or film."

In "Sugar Mama" Ruth Gordon plays an old lady who's not afraid to say exactly what she thinks. "Maybe money doesn't mean that much to me," she tells Alex.

"What's important to me is what I can buy with my money. Nice food. Nice clothes. Nice people."

"MEN ARE SUCH BEASTS"

Episode #12

Synopsis: Tony has been going out with Denise, an attractive girl who is taking speed. He's decided that he wants to stop seeing her, but she refuses to let go of him; Denise even joins the Sunshine Cab Company to be near Tony as much as possible. (Louie is glad to have her around because she's a terrific booker.) Tony tries everything he can think of (short of his boxing skills) to get rid of Denise, yet nothing seems to work. Alex then comes to Tony's rescue: he tells Denise that Tony is in love with someone else. Denise immediately wants to know who the person is—and Tony points out Louie as his lover. Tony tries to convince her that he's gay, but she is highly skeptical. Finally, Denise tells Tony that if he's so desperate he would deny his own masculinity by pretending to be homosexual, then he must really be completely uninterested in her. And Denise gives up on Tony.

Credits: James Burrows directed the script by Stan Daniels and Ed. Weinberger. The guest star was Gail Edwards, as Denise. George Reynolds appeared as a cab driver.

"ELAINE AND THE LAME DUCK"

Episode #13

Synopsis: One night Alex picks up Walter Griswold, a U.S. congressman, in his cab. Despite Walter's powerful position, we learn he is so lacking in self-esteem that he is a total loser with women. After Walter relates some of his depressing experiences, Alex gets the idea that Elaine might be the perfect date for Walter—and Alex takes him to the Sunshine Garage. Elaine and Walter later have dinner at Mario's, but their date consists of one comical disaster after another; Walter even sets his menu on fire accidentally. Yet Elaine goes out with Walter on several occasions: she thinks he's a nice guy, although pity may be one reason she continues to see him. Walter is very pushy with Elaine, wanting their relationship to become more serious at a faster pace than Elaine prefers. Elaine does sleep with the congressman one night, though, and at the end of the episode it appears that their relationship will go on, at least for a while.

Credits: James Burrows directed the script by Glen Charles and Les Charles. Jeffrey Tambor was the guest star, in the role of Walter Griswold. Susan Heldfond appeared as Jill and Rusdi Lane appeared as a waiter.

"BOBBY'S BIG BREAK"

Episode #14

Synopsis: Bobby lands a part in a soap opera, which seems to be a great opportunity for him because it looks as if he'll be working regularly on the soap, entitled *For Better, for Worse*, for quite some time. (Bobby portrays Skip, a former boyfriend of one of the leading characters of *For Better, for Worse.*) Figuring that he'll never have to drive a cab again, Bobby tears up his hack's license. "You better hang on to it," Louie tells him, "because you're gonna need it when you come crawlin' back in here." But Bobby insists that he's a success now and will never return to the garage. "You'll be back, Wheeler," Louie says. "They all come back . . . and when you do, I'll be waitin'. Oooh, will I be waitin'." Unfortunately for Bobby, his character is written out of the soap opera after only two brief appearances: Skip is killed after suffering an accident. Alex is incensed that Louie relishes Bobby's bad luck, and Alex asks Louie to be nice to Bobby when he returns to the garage. At first Louie does act civil toward Bobby, but soon Louie manages to get off a few choice insults.

Credits: James Burrows directed the script by Barry Kemp. Amanda McBroom was the guest star as Olivia, a character on the soap opera, and Michele Conaway played Olivia's friend.

The writer of "Bobby's Big Break," Barry Kemp, comments that "the high point of this episode is when Louie tells Bobby that he better not tear up his hack's license. Louie says, 'You'll be back. Only one guy ever made it out in the whole history of this garage. And that was James Caan. And *he'll* be back.'"

Another note about "Bobby's Big Break": the part of Olivia's friend on the soap opera *For Better, for Worse* was played by Michele Conaway, Jeff Conaway's sister.

"FRIENDS"

Episode #15

Synopsis: Tony entrusts the care of his pet goldfish, George and Wanda, to Bobby while he goes to Scranton for a prize fight. True to form, Bobby forgets to feed the fish, and they die. (When Alex tells him the fish are dead, Bobby says, "Maybe it was one of those murder/ suicide things.") Bobby buys two more goldfish and gives them to Tony when he gets back in town, but Tony is too familiar with his own fish to be fooled. Tony tells the other cabbies, "I know it may seem a little weird to care about them the way I do, but, I mean, to me them fish are like symbols of survival. If them little fish can survive in this world, then so can I." When Tony finds out that George and Wanda are dead, he becomes furious with Bobby. "I don't want to have nothin' to do with you—*friend*," Tony says to Bobby. Bobby is sorry for what he's done. "I hate myself when I do things like that," he says. "Forgettin' things. Not coming through for people." Bobby asks Alex to bring Tony over to his apartment so they can patch things up—and then Bobby forgets about their meeting and brings a girl, Dominque, back to his apartment instead. He tells Alex and Tony that he will break his date, and he goes into the other room to tell Dominique the news—but he never returns. In the end, Tony realizes he has to accept Bobby for what he is.

Credits: James Burrows directed the script by Earl Pomerantz. Liz Miller appeared as Dominique, Bobby's date.

The *New York Times*'s review of "Friends" had this to say: "Tonight *Taxi* explores the touchy subject of close relationships between men in an episode written by Earl Pomerantz. . . . The plot works its way towards reconciliation over steaks and Lowenbrau—'just like in the commercials.' The connection between situation comedies and commercials may be more than superficial. Both forms deal in commodities of basic consumption. *Taxi* happens to be a superior example of its particular genre."

Despite the *Times*'s rather condescending reception, this is an especially fine episode. (Jeff Conaway says this is one of his favorites in the series.) The scene in Bobby's apartment in which Alex and Tony talk about what makes people friends is one of the most poignant moments on *Taxi*.

"LOUIE SEES THE LIGHT"

Episode #16

Synopsis: Louie has been experiencing some severe pains, so he checks into a hospital. He learns that he must undergo exploratory surgery. The cabbies visit Louie in his hopsital room the night before his operation. Louie asks Alex to stay with him after the others have left;

and with Alex as a witness, he pledges to God to be "the best person I can be"—kind, generous, and honest—if he survives the operation. (Alex says to God: "I know he's not your best work.") The doctors find out that Louie's problem is gallstones, and the operation is a complete success—Louie bounces back very quickly. He is determined to keep his pledge to reform his ways, but Bobby bets Alex that Louie won't be able to be nice for one full day. We see that Louie tries hard, but soon his old instincts overpower him. At the end Alex suggests that God may have had a purpose in creating someone as nasty as Louie, that somehow he fits into the scheme of things.

Credits: James Burrows directed the script by Ruth Bennett. Fay Hauser appeared as a nurse, John Dukakis appeared as Goodwin, and J. Alan Thomas appeared as Jeff.

"SUBSTITUTE FATHER"

Episode #17

Synopsis: Elaine asks Alex if he could look after her son, Jason, while she goes

All the guys in the *Taxi* gang get a kick out of babysitting Elaine's son Jason in "Substitute Father."

out of town for a few days. (Elaine has to visit a sick aunt in Buffalo.) Without thinking, Alex says he'll help Elaine out, then realizes he has some other commitments that he can't get out of. So he asks the other guys at the garage to take turns looking after Jason. At first, they're not enthusiastic, but soon they discover that they enjoy being with the boy. Before long, the cabbies are vying for Jason's time, though he is supposed to be studying for the district finals of the national spelling bee. Tony gives Jason boxing lessons, John takes him to the movies, Alex takes him to a Knicks game, and Louie takes him to a wrestling match. Not surprisingly, Jason is too tired the night before the contest to be able to study, and he winds up finishing in second place. Yet he refuses to blame the cabbies for what happened. Jason later tells Elaine, "I'm the one who blew it. Studying was supposed to be my responsibility."

Credits: James Burrows directed the script by Barry Kemp. The guest star was Michael Hershewe, portraying Jason. David Knapp was an official at the spelling bee and Carl Byrd was a parent of one of the contestants.

Barry Kemp, who wrote "Substitute Father," comments that "what I especially remember from that episode is the time when Bobby is feeling awkward and trying to think of something to say to Jason. Bobby asks him, 'So you're a kid, huh?'"

"MAMA GRAVAS"

Episode #18

Synopsis: Latka's mother, Greta Gravas, visits America for the first time. Alex agrees to take Greta out for the evening while Latka has to work at the garage. Greta finds Alex very appealing, and she invites herself over to his apartment, where they spend the night together. The next day Alex explains to Elaine that "I just couldn't help it. When we were alone, she turned into an animal—a *great* one." When Greta tells Latka about what has happened, he assumes that she and Alex will be getting married. Then Greta explains to Latka that she and Alex have no such plans. Latka is stunned to hear this. "If you play *nik-nik* with Alex, you must get married," he says. "It's the only way to save the family honor." Latka soon forgives his mother, though, for he realizes that she needs companionship now that her first husband, Latka's father, has recently died. Yet Latka is adamant about not forgiving Alex. Alex asks Latka to be understanding. "I admit that what your mother and I did was indiscreet," he tells Latka. And Latka replies, "You mean you were not even indoors?" Eventually, Alex and Latka agree to "globnik," which in Latka's country means that they both agree to pretend the whole incident never happened.

Credits: James Burrows directed the script by Glen Charles and Les Charles. Susan Kellermann was the guest star, in the role of Greta Gravas.

Alex says he's quitting the cab business in "Alex Tastes Death and Finds a Nice Restaurant."

"Mama Gravas" is a pretty odd episode. The idea of Alex going to bed with Latka's mother, who can barely speak English, is as strange a premise as any we're presented with on *Taxi*. Some of the goings-on here do seem unconvincing, but there are a few funny moments, too. For instance, at one point Greta and Alex are talking about Latka's father:

Greta: My husband died in the struggle for liberty and freedom.
Alex: So he was a freedom fighter shot by the police?
Greta: No, he was a policeman shot by a freedom fighter.

"ALEX TASTES DEATH AND FINDS A NICE RESTAURANT"

Episode #19

Synopsis: Alex's ear is nearly shot off in a holdup attempt one night in his cab. The bullet nicks Alex's ear, and his hearing is damaged temporarily. The incident upsets him so much he tells everyone in the garage that he's going to quit being a cab driver. He takes a job as a waiter in an elegant French restaurant, and soon afterwards the cabbies go to visit him at his new job. They tell him how much they miss him, and they ask him to come back, but they're distressed to find that he is making a lot more money as a waiter than he did as a cabbie. Alex weighs the pros and cons of the jobs—and finally decides that he wants to return to the Sunshin Cab Company.

Credits: James Burrows directed the script by Michael Leeson. James Stanley played the priest and John Petlock played a waiter. Charles Thomas Murphy and Mavis Palmer were customers at the restaurant.

Judd Hirsch does an outstanding job in this episode of conveying Alex's paranoia about driving a cab again after getting shot. "Picking up total strangers in the middle of the night and driving them wherever they tell you isn't exactly sane," Alex tells the other cabbies.

The best scene of all is the one in which Alex picks up a priest. Alex is so apprehensive about his passengers that he demands that the priest name all twelve apostles; Alex wants proof that he really is a man of the cloth. And when the priest succeeds in thinking of only eleven of them, Alex drives him out of his cab with a baseball bat. "That was a close call," he says.

make use of. He treats them to champagne and good food. He promises Bobby a part in the film. Most of the cabbies are glad to cooperate with Chapman, yet Alex is at first reluctant because he feels a need to protect his privacy. After more persuasion from Chapman and from the other cabbies, however, Alex decides to cooperate on the project. The cab drivers are all convinced they're going to be part of a hit movie, but in the end there's a change of executives at the production company, and the movie is canceled. The cab drivers then feel that they have been used.

Credits: James Burrows directed the script by Glen Charles and Les Charles. The guest star was Martin Mull, as Roger Chapman. Joey Aresco played Michael Patrese.

"Hollywood Calling" is enhanced by Martin Mull's performance as Roger Chapman. Mull, best known for his appearances on *Fernwood Tonight,* has a very sure touch as the egotistical director who's able to twist all of the cabbies around his finger.

"HOLLYWOOD CALLING"

Episode #20

Synopsis: A movie company comes to the Sunshine Garage to make a film about cab drivers. The director of the film, Roger Chapman, pumps the cabbies for experiences they can recall that he could

"MEMORIES OF CAB 804, PART I"

Episode #21

Synopsis: John Burns wrecks Cab 804, the oldest in the fleet. (The cab has logged nearly half a million miles.) As Latka musters all his abilities in trying to save it, the drivers reminisce about some of the memorable things that have happened in Cab 804. Alex remembers that he was driving that cab the night he first met John. Alex picked John up near Grand Central Station just after he had arrived in New York from Texas; we learn that John had recently been rejected by a girl he wanted to marry. To get change for a fifty-dollar bill, Alex took John to the Sunshine Garage. (We see John and Alex coming into the garage together at the beginning of "Like Father, Like Daughter.") A few days later John joined the cab company. Bobby recalls the night he thwarted a guy who tried to hold him up. Bobby and the would-be thief spent a long time attempting to out-bluff each other. And Tony recalls the night a man told him to stop the cab halfway across the Brooklyn Bridge so that he could jump. Tony convinced him not to commit suicide. (Tony said, "Don't do that." And the man replied, "OK.")

Credits: James Burrows directed the script by Barry Kemp. Scoey Mitchell played the part of the thief.

The segment that shows how Alex and John first met was originally intended for the pilot episode, "Like Father, Like Daughter." "The first show was way too long," recalls Randall Carver. "It could have been a two-parter. They were trying to introduce all the characters and their past stories. Lots of scenes, like the one where I got into Alex's cab, were shot for the first episode and weren't used at all or were used later."

The writer of this episode, Barry Kemp, says that "the scenes showing the interiors of the cabs were always shot on the stage—with the single exception of one sequence in 'Memories of Cab 804.'

This was the sequence with Tony and the guy who was going to jump off the bridge. That was actually shot in New York—the reason we could do that was because the script was written early enough so that when the second unit went out to shoot in New York [to get exterior shots of cabs driving into and out of the garage], we already knew that that scene would be used on the show."

Jeff Conaway recalls that the segments of "Memories of Cab 804" were filmed at various times during the first season. "If there was time after we did one of the earlier episodes, we'd shoot another segment of the show about Cab 804 at the end of the night. . . . It was a way of getting more work done in less time." He also remembers that when he auditioned for *Taxi*, he did a reading from Bobby's segment of "Memories of Cab 804," as well as some scenes from the pilot episode.

"MEMORIES OF CAB 804, PART II"

Episode #22

Synopsis: The *Taxi* gang continues to reminisce about Cab 804. Alex remembers the night when a young woman had a baby in the cab. Her husband panicked (in spite of his knowledge of the Lamaze Method), and Alex was forced to be the one to help the woman give birth. Louie remembers a rich boy who got into the cab with an envelope containing six hundred dollars. The boy, a real brat, told Louie that his father had said, "This money is not for gambling." Yet the kid then tricked Louie into some sucker bets. In the end, however, Louie won the whole six hundred dollars from him. And Elaine recalls the time she drove a fare to an art auction 140 miles out in the country. Elaine found the man she picked up in Cab 804 that night, Mike Brandon, to be irresistible—he was handsome, successful, and well-mannered—and he asked her to spend the night with him. Elaine was very tempted, but she felt she couldn't go through with it because he wouldn't promise anything about the future. After she returned to the garage, Bobby told her, "The guy had to have a flaw somewhere." "Yeah," Elaine replied, "He took 'no' for an answer." At the end of the episode, Latka appears to have finally put Cab 804 back into working order. Yet when Alex gets in and turns the ignition, smoke starts pouring out of the engine. "On reflection," Alex comments, "I think maybe I delivered that baby in Cab 803."

Credits: James Burrows directed the script by Barry Kemp. Tom Selleck appeared as Mike Brandon, Chris Barnes appeared as the rich boy, and Mandy Patinkin and Regi Baff were the young man and woman in Alex's cab.

Elaine's segment in this episode has some of Marilu Henner's best moments of the series. In this touching vignette, in which Elaine meets her "perfect man" (well played by Tom Selleck, who's best known for his starring role on *Magnum, P.I.*), Marilu conveys Elaine's predicament with a fine sense of understatement. We see that Elaine really wants to be seduced by Mike. "You're not perfect after all," Elaine says to him. "You don't even know when to lie."

Barry Kemp recalls that "the idea for 'Memories of Cab 804' came from Studs Terkel's book *Working.* He had a section in there on cab drivers, and he said that every driver had a favorite cab. So we thought, 'What if their favorite cab was wrecked?'"

"HONOR THY FATHER"

Episode #23

Synopsis: Alex's sister Charlotte arrives at the garage looking for her brother, and she reveals that their father has been admitted to a nearby hospital. Alex takes the news with indifference (to the dismay of Bobby, Elaine, and Tony), because he still blames his father for deserting him thirty years ago. Finally, Charlotte persuades Alex to visit the hospital, where Alex mistakes a sickly, dying man for his father. Alex's father, Joe, on the other hand, is recuperating pretty well, and father and son seem, by the end of the episode, to be on their way towards becoming less antagonistic to each other.

Credits: James Burrows directed the script by Glen Charles and Les Charles. Joan Hackett played Charlotte, Jack Gilford played Joe, and Ian Wolfe played the dying man.

Most of what occurs in "Honor Thy Father" actually happened to James Brooks. Brooks recalls that, like Alex, he once mistook another man for his father in the hospital. Plus, it was Brooks's sis-

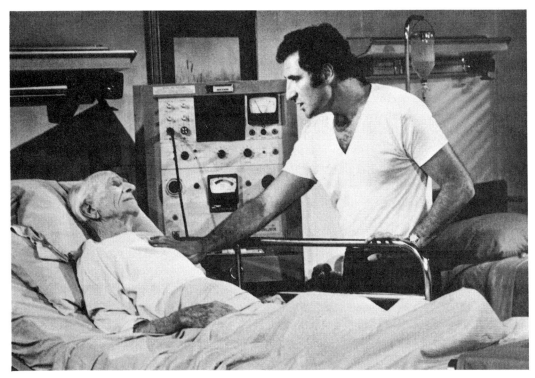

Alex mistakes a dying man for his father in "Honor Thy Father."

ter who forced him to visit his father for the first time in many years.

This episode was nominated for an Emmy Award for outstanding writing in a comedy series.

"THE RELUCTANT FIGHTER"

Episode #24

Synopsis: Tony is elated when he lands a fight with Benny Foster, a former champion; for once, Tony receives lots of attention in the press. But Tony is disturbed when he finds out that Foster is only coming out of retirement to win some money to pay for an operation for Brian Sims, a boy who's been confined to a wheelchair. Tony realizes that he can't win, no matter what happens in the fight. Louie makes him feel even worse when he says to Tony, "I'm glad you're fighting this fight. Every time I bet against you, I clean up. You've paid for my whole living room." Tony's dilemma is that if he loses, Louie will get to gloat over him—yet if Tony wins, Brian will be seriously disappointed, and possibly never get a chance to walk again. Tony decides to give it his best shot in the ring, however, and he manages to beat the ex-champ. At the end of the episode Brian forgives Tony for beating his fighter, and Tony agrees to box for Brian in the future. "I'll stick

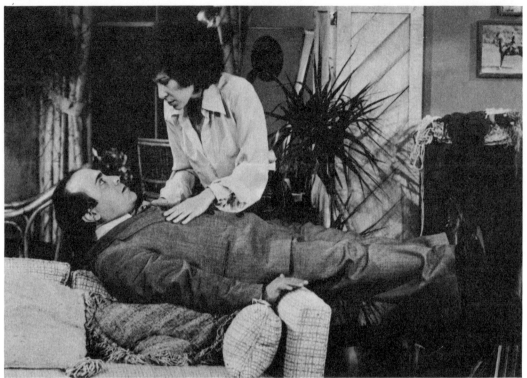

Zena Sherman seduces Louie at the end of "Louie and the Nice Girl."

around until you lose," Brian tells Tony.

Credits: James Burrows directed the script by Ken Estin. Marc Danza was the guest star, in the role of Brian Sims. Armando Muniz played Benny Foster, Michael V. Gazzo played Vince, and Gene Le Bell played the referee.

Tony Danza's son Marc makes his first appearance on *Taxi* in this episode. (Marc returns in Episode #37, entitled "Tony and Brian.") Tony and his son work together well on *Taxi.* They make a point of avoiding sentimentality—in fact, most of the time they're fighting. Marc Danza's character is almost always acting tough and abrasive.

SECOND-SEASON CREDITS

Alex Rieger—Judd Hirsch
Elaine Nardo—Marilu Henner
Louie DePalma—Danny DeVito
Tony Banta—Tony Danza
Jim Ignatowski—Christopher Lloyd
Bobby Wheeler—Jeff Conaway
Latka Gravas—Andy Kaufman

Executive Producers—James Brooks, Stan Daniels, and Ed. Weinberger
Producers—Glen Charles and Les Charles
Executive Script Consultant—Barry Kemp

Executive Story Editor—David Lloyd
Story Editors—Howard Gewirtz and
Ian Praiser
Program Consultant—Ken Estin
Associate Producer—Richard Sakai
Executive Consultant—James
Brooks
Director—James Burrows
Film Editor—M. Pam Blumenthal
Art Director—Lynn Griffin
Director of Photography—Edward
Nugent
Unit Production Manager—Gregg
Peters
Music—Bob James

"LOUIE AND THE NICE GIRL"

Episode #25

Synopsis: Zena Sherman, who refills
the vending machines at the garage, reveals a desire to go out with Louie—because she is "intrigued by men of power."
Elaine, Bobby, and Tony shudder at the
prospect of introducing such a nice
woman to such a vicious guy, but Alex
sees nothing wrong and helps to fix Louie
and Zena up. Zena and Louie then start
seeing each other regularly. The cabbies'
dismay grows as lecherous Louie brags
about his conquest of Zena: Louie claims
that he and Zena have a great sex life. But
one day Zena comes to the garage and
asks to speak to Alex about a problem
she's having. She reveals to Alex that
Louie has never even made a pass at her;

she can't understand why he doesn't
seem to find her sexually desirable. Later,
when Louie tries to brag about his sexual
prowess, Alex informs him that he knows
what's really going on. Then Louie admits to Alex that he can't seem to be able
to get romantic with a "nice" girl like
Zena. (His previous experience apparently has been exclusively with women of
the sleaziest kind.) Louie says to Alex
that he has decided he will break off his
relationship with Zena, and he goes to
Zena's apartment to tell her the news.
She gets Louie to admit to her about how
he has always divided women into "nice"
girls and "bad" girls. Zena kisses Louie,
and at the end of the episode she succeeds
in seducing him.

Credits: James Burrows directed the
script by Earl Pomerantz. Rhea Perlman
was the guest star, in the role of Zena
Sherman.

In a review of this episode, *Variety*
commented, "The script mixed mirth
and pathos in equal portions as DeVito's
bragging camouflaged a pathetic inability
to respond to 'the first girl I ever went out
with twice in my life.' DeVito and Perlman deftly moved from bellylaughs to
heartbreak, with DeVito adroitly running
the gamut from being obnoxious to being
genuinely pathetic."

Rhea Perlman made her first appearance on *Taxi* in "Louie and the Nice
Girl." When this episode was filmed in
1979, she was Danny DeVito's real-life
girlfriend. (They weren't married until
two years later.)

Another note of interest: "Louie and
the Nice Girl" won an Emmy for James

Burrows in 1980 for outstanding directing in a comedy series.

"WHEREFORE ART THOU BOBBY?"

Episode #26

Synopsis: Tony brings Steve Jensen, a young guy from Iowa who's just arrived in New York, to the garage in order to meet Bobby. Tony hopes that Bobby will be able to advise Steve on how he might go about becoming an actor. Steve gets an audition, and, surprisingly, he is immediately chosen to play Romeo in an important off-Broadway production. When Louie hears about Steve's good fortune (which is sure to make Bobby jealous), he wants to be the one to tell Bobby what has happened. And after Bobby finds out about Steve's big break, Bobby says he wants to quit acting. But when he helps Steve out by rehearsing a scene from *Romeo and Juliet* with him, Bobby gets involved in the scene so intensely that he realizes that he must continue to try to become an actor. Furthermore, Bobby wants to deprive Louie of the satisfaction of knowing he's given up on his dreams. Bobby tells Louie, "One day I'm gonna come back in here and shove every word you've said down your throat."

Credits: James Burrows directed the script by Barry Kemp. The guest star was Michael Horton, portraying Steve Jensen.

"REVEREND JIM: A SPACE ODYSSEY"

Episode #27

Synopsis: The cabbies see Reverend Jim at Mario's and recall that he married Latka to an American girl the year before. Jim is a lost soul, spending most of his time in bars, when Elaine, Alex, Bobby, and Tony decide to help him out of his stupor. In a crash program, they get him to pass his written test for a hack's license, and he joins the gang at the Sunshine Cab Company.

Credits: James Burrows directed the script by Glen Charles and Les Charles. Kenneth Kimmins was the guest star as a license examiner.

Several members of the cast and crew of *Taxi*, including James Brooks and Christopher Lloyd, say they especially enjoyed making this episode because most of them had personally known sixties dropouts like Jim Ignatowski. "Reverend Jim: A Space Odyssey" features some of Christopher Lloyd's best moments on *Taxi*. Lloyd unerringly hits the right note of good-natured dopiness in the character. The script includes many amusing lines. For instance, Tony angrily says to Jim at one point, "The only reason guys like you got to stay at home and protest and get loaded was because guys like me were over in 'Nam doin' your fightin' for you. What do you say to that?" Jim thinks for a second and answers, "Thank you."

Another memorable sequence in the episode is the one in which Jim takes the

A nervous breakdown can involve many symptoms, but Alex isn't prepared for this one as Elaine comes on to him in "Nardo Loses Her Marbles."

exam for his hack's license. The rest of the gang is watching him as he is baffled by a question on the test. He calls across the room to them and asks, "What does a yellow light mean?" "Slow down," they reply. At first Jim is totally perplexed, then he comes up with the only response he can apparently think of: he repeats the question, more slowly. They give him the same answer again, and he keeps repeating the question with growing desperation as they keep replying, "Slow down." James Burrows remembers that "it was only supposed to go once, but when I saw that the audience was laughing their heads off, I just let it go for as long as I thought they could build on it. That bit wound up running for about a minute and a half."

"NARDO LOSES HER MARBLES"

Episode #28

Synopsis: Elaine is feeling the pressures of holding down two jobs and trying to raise her two children, Jason and Jennifer. Her nerves are on edge, and she has an emotional outburst at an art show, where she threatens to smash an artist's sculpture. Alex sees that Elaine is having some problems and suggests that she go to see a psychiatrist. Alex says to her, "Stop trying to act so tough." Elaine replies, "I'm a single parent with two kids to take care of. I've got to be tough." At first Elaine refuses to visit the psychiatrist, and instead she offers to sleep with Alex. Alex declines, saying that she is only flirting with him to avoid facing her problems. Reluctantly, Elaine goes to a psychiatrist, and the visit comes off so well that she agrees to start seeing him regularly. Elaine thanks Alex for not taking advantage of her when she was distressed and had offered to go to bed with him. "Yeah," Alex responds. "it's a good thing that one of us had the sense to stop from doing something . . . that we would have both remembered fondly for the rest of our lives."

Credits: James Burrows directed the script by Earl Pomerantz. Tom Ewell was the guest star, in the role of the psychiatrist, Dr. Henry Collins, while Paula Victor played Mrs. Hazeltine, Mary Woronov played Fran, Robert Picardo played Philip, and William Callaway played Sandor Kovacs.

"A WOMAN BETWEEN FRIENDS"

Episode #29

Synopsis: Tony and Bobby meet a pretty girl named Janet at Mario's, and they both become interested in her. For a while, they each take Janet out on dates, and they seem to be on the verge of fight-

ing over her like adolescents. Bobby says, "As far as Janet's concerned, it's war." Yet Bobby and Tony soon realize they don't want to spoil their friendship. Their solution is to demand that Janet chose between them. Before she can give them her preference, though, they tell her they don't want to hear it: for if she picks one of them, the other one will be hurt. Bobby and Tony inform her that they both want to stop seeing her. Janet is not happy about this, and she lets them know she was going to make the guy she preferred "very glad that he was a man tonight." As she walks away from them for the last time, Janet says that Bobby was going to be her choice.

Credits: James Burrows directed the script by Ken Estin. Constance Forslund was the guest star as Janet. T. J. Castronova played Tommy, the bartender, and Mike Binder played an actor.

We learn quite a lot in this episode about Bobby's prowess with women. At one point Tony talks about how he admires Bobby's skills. "He's got a million great lines," Tony says, "and they all work." Furthermore, Elaine tells Bobby that "you don't pay attention to women, you collect them."

"THE LIGHTER SIDE OF ANGELA MATUSA"

Episode #30

Synopsis: The cabbies hear again from Angela Matusa, the overweight girl who

Angela expects Alex to fall in love with her in "The Lighter Side of Angela Matusa."

was once Alex's blind date. Louie remarks, "Some men try to climb mountains, others just date them." Yet when we see Angela we discover that she has lost a hundred pounds—now she's svelte and sexy. She explains that her determination to stick to her diet was based on the assumption that Alex would fall in love with her if she were thinner. When Alex lets her know he's still not romantically interested in her, she becomes depressed and starts eating heavily again. But Alex manages to convince her not to gain back the weight she lost. He brings her together with a guy, Wayne, who is attracted to her. Alex is happy for Angela and Wayne, but at the end he finds out that Wayne is married and has children.

Credits: James Burrows directed the script by Earl Pomerantz. Suzanne Kent was the guest star as Angela Matusa. Phil Rubenstein appeared as Wayne, Dick Miller appeared as Ernie, and T. J.

Castronova appeared as Tommy, the bartender.

"THE GREAT RACE"

Episode #31

Synopsis: Louie brags to the cabbies about what a great taxi driver he used to be. He makes fun of Bobby's low bookings, saying he used to make a lot more money. Bobby then challenges Louie to a bet: that Alex (the best cabbie now driving for the Sunshine Company) can bring in more money than Louie in a particular shift. The prize for the winner is to be a date with Elaine (who naturally shudders at the prospect of going out with Louie). So it's Alex versus Louie in a tough contest to see who can book the most. In the end Louie gets more money on the meter,

Louie hopes to win a date with Elaine in "The Great Race."

but Alex brings in more money if tips are also counted. Latka judges the contest, and he says that tips should count. Alex is declared the winner of the contest.

Credits: James Burrows directed the script by Glenn Gordon Caron. Scott Brady appeared as Inspector Melnick, Bob Levine appeared as a businessman, Jean Owens Hayworth appeared as an old lady, and J. Alan Thomas appeared as Jeff.

Glenn Gordon Caron, who wrote the script for "The Great Race," has recently become famous for being the creator of *Moonlighting*.

"THE APARTMENT"

Episode #32

Synopsis: Latka's apartment building is scheduled to be torn down, and he must find a new home. He rents a luxurious penthouse for three thousand dollars— his life's savings. Latka doesn't realize that he'll have to come up with that amount every month to stay in his plush apartment. When they learn about Latka's ridiculous choice of a place to live, the cabbies tell him he's got to get out of his lease as fast as he can. Alex visits the apartment and he's completely bowled over by it. "This apartment is for people like the Vanderbilts, the Rockefellers, the Bee Gees," he says. Soon the cabbies succumb to the luxury of the place: the great view, the Jacuzzi, the maid service, and the comfortable fur-

niture. Everybody in the gang enjoys living it up at Latka's apartment. They organize a rent party to raise enough money to keep the apartment for another month. No women, except for Elaine, show up at the party, though, and all the men who arrive demand their money back. With the failure of the party, the cabbies realize they'll have to leave the place at the end of the month. As he looks around the apartment for the last time, Latka says, "Good-bye, panoramic view."

Credits: James Burrows directed the script by Barry Rubinowitz. Nancy Steen appeared as the maid. Dick Butkus was Don and Mike Binder was an actor— both were guests at the party.

Barry Kemp, who was the executive script consultant for *Taxi* at the time "The Apartment" was made, remembers, "There were so many mechanical failures with cameras when we tried to film this episode that we had to go over to the sets of other series in order to find enough cameras to shoot our show. Lots of times on *Taxi* things would be changing or going wrong right up to the minute we started shooting. . . . Sometimes we didn't know ahead of time if something was going to come off or not."

"ELAINE'S SECRET ADMIRER"

Episode #33

Synopsis: Elaine begins receiving anonymous love poems, and she finds them very romantic. Jim admits to Alex that he is the one responsible for writing the poetry. (Jim wants to cheer up Elaine, who's been feeling depressed lately.) Meanwhile, another cabbie, Dennis, tells Elaine that he is the poet, and they begin going out together. In the end, though, Jim proves to Elaine that he is really the one who's been sending her the love letters. And he gives her an unusual gift: a miniature castle made up of pieces of metal taken from his van. Elaine is touched by Jim's gesture, though she isn't interested in him romantically, of course.

Credits: James Burrows directed the script by Barry Kemp.

"ALEX'S ROMANCE"

Episode #34

Synopsis: Bobby introduces Alex to Joyce Rogers, an actress who has just been dropped from a part on a soap opera. At first Alex just tries to cheer her up, but he soon begins romancing her. Although they had agreed not to get serious about each other, Alex and Joyce have a passionate affair that lasts for two weeks. Alex even raises the subject of marriage, but Joyce doesn't feel that it would work out for them. Furthermore, she gets an offer to go to Los Angeles and star in a pilot for a TV series. In the end Alex says, "We're fighting because we care about each other, but we're breaking up because we don't care enough."

Credits: Ed. Weinberger directed the

script by Ian Praiser and Howard Gewirtz. The guest star was Dee Wallace, playing the part of Joyce Rogers.

Ian Praiser, one of the producers of the series during the later seasons, says he and his writing partner Howard Gewirtz were put on the staff of *Taxi* because of their script for "Alex's Romance." "We wrote this episode on spec during the first season and sent it to David Davis," Praiser remembers. "We got work right away from it, but not for *Taxi*. . . . Next season, I called Stan Daniels and asked him what had happened to the episode. Daniels had never read it, but he said then that he would. And he gave the script to Jim Brooks. They both liked it and they offered us a story editorship with the show. Suddenly, we were on *Taxi*. You rise so quickly in this business, sometimes you feel as though you've got the bends."

Alex's affair with Joyce Rogers (portrayed by Dee Wallace, who has gone on to star in *E.T.* and other movies) includes several poignant moments. The scene in which Joyce rejects Alex's proposal is especially memorable: he tries, without much success, to conceal his feeling of disappointment.

"LATKA'S REVOLTING"

Episode #35

Synopsis: Latka learns that a revolution is going on in his homeland. He asks Alex for advice about whether he should return to fight in the revolution. (Latka is a general in the rebel army.) Latka has made up his mind to go when an old friend, Baschi Krepitz, from his home country arrives in town. Baschi, who is also a rebel, reports to Latka about the situation back home. Baschi explains that the rebel forces are hopelessly outnumbered and surrounded, and Latka realizes that to go home now would be suicidal— and that there is a difference between loyalty and idiocy. Instead of departing for his homeland, Latka says he has something more important to do: watching *The Tonight Show*.

Credits: James Burrows directed the script by Glen Charles and Les Charles. The guest star was Lenny Baker, playing Baschi Krepitz. Also appearing was T. J. Castronova, as Tommy, the bartender.

"LOUIE MEETS THE FOLKS"

Episode #36

Synopsis: Zena Sherman lets Louie know that he must agree to meet her parents or she'll break off their relationship. Afraid (and with good cause, we realize) that Zena's parents won't like him, Louie pays Alex two hundred dollars to come along with him to the Shermans'. We learn that Zena's parents are very strait-laced; in fact, her father is a minister. The Reverend and Mrs. Sherman are appalled at Louie's manners (or lack thereof) and behavior. To make matters worse, Louie explains to them that "before I met Zena, my longest relationship had lasted

about thirty minutes." Mrs. Sherman is shocked to the point that she informs Louie she'll have him killed if he ever tries to marry Zena. (She tells Louie, "It'll be our little secret.")

Credits: James Burrows directed the script by Barry Kemp. Rhea Perlman was the guest star as Zena Sherman, with John C. Becher and Camila Ashland as the Reverend and Mrs. Sherman.

Barry Kemp, who wrote "Louie Meets the Folks," recalls, "The idea for this episode was Jim Brooks's. He wanted Zena's mother to deliver to Louie a great speech about how you would go about killing someone. And I had to try and make it believable that the wife of this minister could convince Louie she really would pay someone to do away with him. The whole episode was set up to lead to that moment."

"TONY AND BRIAN"

Episode #37

Synopsis: Tony wants to adopt Brian, a nine-year-old boy whom he has befriended. But Brian has other ideas: he's staying with a wealthy family from Scarsdale, who he hopes will soon agree to adopt him. (Brian had earlier been hanging out at playgrounds where there were kids with rich parents.) Alex is disturbed to hear about Brian's preference. "I'm mad that his kid has perverted values, that money counts for everything in this world—and that I don't have any," comments Alex. Brian gets an unpleasant surprise when the rich family decides not to adopt him. He then goes back to Tony and says he's now willing to live with him after all. Tony is disappointed to be the boy's second choice, yet he does consent to adopt Brian.

Credits: James Burrows directed the script by Ken Estin. Marc Danza was the guest star, in the role of Brian Sims.

A particularly funny scene in this episode occurs when Bobby mentions that an extremely negative review of one of his performances (as Biff in *Death of a Salesman*) has been published in a Long Island newspaper. "At least no one reads that lousy rag," Bobby tells the other cabbies. At that moment Louie wheels in a cart that's filled with copies of the newspaper in question.

"Tony and Brian" is the last episode in which Tony Danza's son Marc makes an appearance. Although there are a few references to Brian in the episodes immediately following this one, the character seems to have been totally forgotten later in the series. For instance, in "Tony's Baby," a fifth-season episode in which Tony gets his girlfriend Vicki pregnant, we hear no mention at all of the fact that Tony is supposed to have a son already.

of gambling. Still, Jim is not about to stop going to the track, even if he has to borrow money from Louie (at an exorbitant interest rate). After losing heavily at first, Jim's fortunes dramatically change for the better when he wins big on a horse named On Dasher, a three-hundred-to-one long shot. Everyone else in the *Taxi* gang is amazed to learn that Jim has used his winnings to buy On Dasher, a tired old nag. (Jim changes the horse's name to Gary because he feels that On Dasher was his "slave name.") Reverend Jim treats Gary as if he were a house pet, taking him for walks in the park and allowing him to sleep in his apartment. But Gary soon becomes ill and dies in bed at Jim's place. Reverend Jim delivers a eulogy for his pet.

Credits: James Burrows directed the script by David Lloyd.

A highlight of this episode is the scene in which Alex does a funny little skit about gambling. Alex attempts to convince Jim that gambling has a negative side, and to illustrate his point Alex briefly plays several parts: a Mafia loan collector, a policeman, and a neighbor of the Ignatowskis'.

"JIM GETS A PET"

Episode #38

Synopsis: We learn that Reverend Jim enjoys betting on the horses, in spite of admonitions from Elaine about the evils

"WHAT PRICE BOBBY?"

Episode #39

Synopsis: Bobby, hoping to meet an important producer or agent, regularly cruises the theater district in his cab; one night he picks up Nora Chandliss, a man-

Bobby learns that his new manager, Nora Chandliss, is interested in him for more than just his acting talents in "What Price Bobby?"

ager of some big-name actors, as a fare. Bobby tries to convince her to come to Brooklyn and watch the play he's currently appearing in. She says she will, although Bobby suspects that she is just being polite. He's in for a jolt when she not only shows up at the theater a few days later to see his performance, but offers to take him on as a client as well. Nora even pays for Bobby to get a new wardrobe and a new hairstyle. The catch is that she expects Bobby to sleep with her. He does, but he soon feels uneasy

about the whole arrangement. Elaine asks Bobby, "Come on, it's not like you're prostituting yourself. Is it?" And from Bobby's reaction, we see that he feels he is. Bobby eventually works up the nerve to tell Nora that he wants to end their personal relationship and have exclusively a business relationship. She rewards his honesty by dropping him as a client.

Credits: James Burrows directed the script by Ken Estin. The guest star was Susan Sullivan, in the role of Nora Chandliss.

An especially memorable sequence in "What Price Bobby?" occurs near the end of the episode. Nora Chandliss has just told Bobby to get out of her apartment. He then says to her, "OK, so I lost my manager. I lost my job. I lost my future. I lost my self-respect. But at least I have one thing left—I have my shoes. . . . They were the only thing I could think of. But they're mine." Then Nora humiliates Bobby further by telling him she'll take him back if he gives her his shoes. He does—and she reacts by telling him to get out and never return.

"GUESS WHO'S COMING FOR BREFNISH?"

Episode #40

Synopsis: Simka Dahblitz applies for a job as a secretary at the Sunshine Cab Company, and Latka overhears her speaking their native language. Immediately they hit it off romantically, but Simka confides to the cabbies that she fears her relationship with Latka will be over once he finds out she is a "mountain person." (Latka is a "lowlands person," and in the home country the two factions are bitter enemies.) The cabbies persuade her to tell Latka the truth, and he is clearly displeased to hear it. Simka then starts dating John, an old boyfriend of hers.

Credits: James Burrows directed the script by Barry Kemp. The guest star was Carol Kane, portraying Simka Dahblitz. Frank Ashmore appeared as John Hannon.

This episode marks the first appearance of Carol Kane on *Taxi*.

"SHUT IT DOWN, PART I"

Episode #41

Synopsis: Tony is nearly killed when the brakes go out on his cab. All of the cabbies are furious that the company is making them drive cars that are nearly falling apart. They elect Elaine as shop steward, and she makes their grievances known to Louie and Mr. MacKenzie, the owner of the Sunshine Cab Company. Louie and Mr. MacKenzie refuse to do anything, so the cabbies vote to go on strike. The cabbies spend several freezing days on a picket line. Meanwhile, Louie hires a group of boys and old men as drivers. The union has set a date to hold a

hearing on the cabbies' grievances, but Louie has doctored the books to make it look as if the Sunshine Cab Company has been spending more on maintenance than any other taxi company. Alex says, "Louie, when you walk into that hearing room, you're going to be under oath. You know what that means?" "Yeah," Louie replies. "It means they gotta believe you. I love this country." Finally, Louie comes up with a solution to end the strike: he'll agree to give in to the union's demands if Elaine goes out with him on a date. Very reluctantly, she agrees.

Credits: James Burrows directed the script by Howard Gewirtz and Ian Praiser, from a story by Mark Jacobson and Michael Tolkin.

"'Shut It Down' was meant to be a one-parter," explains Ian Praiser. "It was James Brooks who suggested Louie's pact with Elaine—and that turned it into a two-parter. Their date was too big an issue to be dealt with in one episode. We started that week on Monday with a one-part script and by Friday the actors had to absorb all the changes and additions that made it a two-parter. I think it was a good episode, especially because of the chemistry between Marilu and Danny."

"SHUT IT DOWN, PART II"

Episode #42

Synopsis: Elaine agrees to Louie's scheme to meet the cabbies' demands if she goes out with him. As could be expected, Louie gloats over the prospect of dating Elaine. Alex tells him, "You try anything with Elaine and I'll kill you." To which Louie replies, "It'll take the coroner a week to pry the grin off my face." When the time comes for Louie to pick Elaine up, we see that she has protected herself by wearing several layers of sweaters and heavy coats. They have dinner and go dancing (though Elaine has to bend over in order to dance with him). Louie brings her back to the door of her apartment and begs for a good-night kiss. She finally gives him one—and he grabs her and tries, without success, to get much more than just a kiss from her.

Credits: James Burrows directed the script by Howard Gewirtz and Ian Praiser, from a story by Mark Jacobson and Michael Tolkin.

Bobby imagines becoming a big rock star who refuses to admit ever having known Louie. Reverend Jim's fantasy is being taken by aliens for a ride on a spaceship. At the end, Herve Villechaize stops by the garage, picks up his photographs, and watches Louie do an impression of his character from *Fantasy Island*.

Credits: James Burrows directed the script by Barry Kemp. Herve Villechaize and Eric Sevareid were the guest stars, playing themselves.

"Jim's segment of 'Fantasy Borough' posed a major problem for our art director," remembers Ian Praiser. "It was difficult to rig the amount of lights that were necessary to shine into Jim's apartment from the alien ship. And for Jim to be able to walk out onto the rigging of the spacecraft, the art director used a lot of Styrofoam and painted it all gray."

"FANTASY BOROUGH, PART I"

Episode #43

Synopsis: Herve Villechaize, one of the stars of *Fantasy Island*, accidentally leaves some photos in Tony's cab one day. Tony calls Villechaize at his hotel, and he says he'll come to the garage in person to pick up the photos. While they wait for him to arrive, we see what each of the cabbies fantasizes about. Tony, tired of being called dumb, envisions picking up Eric Sevareid and impressing him with his intellectual prowess. Latka imagines being the dispatcher at the Sunshine Cab Company, with Louie as his mechanic. (Latka also has Louie sent before a firing squad.)

"FANTASY BOROUGH, PART II"

Episode #44

Synopsis: The cabbies continue to reveal their fantasies. Alex envisions meeting a beautiful girl in his cab who falls for him. He takes the girl of his dreams to his apartment, where they sit before a fire sipping brandy. They're about to make love when they find out that Alex is her long-lost uncle. (Something always goes wrong in Alex's fantasies, we learn.) Louie imagines being fabulously rich and married to Elaine. Louie also imagines owning the Sunshine Cab Company and

In "Fantasy Borough," Louie imagines the pleasures of being married to Elaine.

having Lassie for a pet. Elaine's fantasy is to turn the drab garage into the setting for a scene from a Broadway musical. The cabbies form a chorus line and dance to "Lullaby of Broadway," backed by an orchestra. The guys are dressed in tuxedos, with top hats and canes.

Credits: James Burrows directed the script by Barry Kemp. The girl in Alex's fantasy was played by Priscilla Barnes. Lassie made a cameo appearance.

The "Lullaby of Broadway" song-and-dance sequence was done mainly to please Marilu Henner, who had often asked the producers to "figure out a way to get some singing and dancing into the show."

"ART WORK"

Episode #45

Synopsis: Elaine criticizes the other cabbies for their habit of gambling. She tells them, "Every day at that gallery I see rich people getting richer by investing in art. They gamble, but they always win." The cabbies realize that if they were to pool their money, they could afford to buy a work of art. Elaine knows of a painting by an artist, Max Duffin, that's likely to go up in value soon because the artist isn't expected to live much longer. "Buying one of the old geezer's paintings is like bettin' he's gonna die," says Louie. "We can't lose." The rest of the gang is wary, but they decide they need to bring Louie into the deal in order to put together enough money for the painting. They go to the art auction where Duffin's work is being sold, but they are outbid by someone who offers twenty-nine hundred dollars for the painting. Right after the bidding ends, it's announced that Max Duffin has died, which means that the painting has already increased in value to at least five thousand dollars. To console themselves, each of the cabbies buys an inexpensive work of art at the gallery.

Credits: James Burrows directed the script by Glen Charles and Les Charles. Marvin Newman was the guest star, in the role of the auctioneer.

At one point in this episode Jim stuns everyone by reciting, from memory, Rudyard Kipling's poem "If." It's very funny that Reverend Jim, who can barely cope with the simplest task (like filling out a job application form), has some sur-

Bobby talks to Alex just before the climax of "Alex Jumps Out of an Airplane."

prising talents. For instance, besides his knowledge of literature, Jim speaks French and plays the piano well.

"ALEX JUMPS OUT OF AN AIRPLANE"

Episode #46

Synopsis: At Mario's, Alex tells the other cabbies about his latest ski weekend. He recalls that in order to impress an attractive woman, he went off a ski jump, even though he'd never jumped before. When Elaine asks him why he didn't explain to the woman that he had no experience ski jumping, Alex replies, "Did I tell you she had the bluest eyes I ever saw?" "Say no more," Bobby says before Elaine can respond. Alex explains that when he jumped, it turned out to be "the biggest thrill of my life." So, Alex has decided, "the most important thing in a man's life is to face his fears." Alex becomes a daredevil—for a while. First, he gets Tony to agree to give him boxing lessons, then he plays the piano and sings in front of an audience at Mario's, and finally he decides to conquer his greatest fear: jumping out of a plane. Though terrified of heights, he manages to make his parachute jump.

Credits: James Burrows directed the script by Ken Estin. T. J. Castronova appeared as Tommy and Beverly Ross appeared as the woman sky-diving instructor.

Viewers will savor Hirsch's superb work here: it's the best piece of acting in the series. When Alex tells the other cabbies about his ski-jumping experience, Hirsch makes the scene seem so vivid that we feel almost as if we had been there with him on the ski slopes, even though all we've actually seen is Alex talking at Mario's. How many other actors on television could hold an audience's attention so commandingly throughout such a long speech? Hirsch's acting, plus an excellent script by Ken Estin, makes this possibly the finest episode of *Taxi*.

THIRD-SEASON CREDITS
Alex Rieger—Judd Hirsch
Elaine Nardo—Marilu Henner
Louie DePalma—Danny DeVito
Tony Banta—Tony Danza
Jim Ignatowski—Christopher Lloyd
Bobby Wheeler—Jeff Conaway
Latka Gravas—Andy Kaufman

Executive Producers—James Brooks, Stan Daniels, and Ed. Weinberger
Producers—Glen Charles and Les Charles
Executive Script Consultant—Barry Kemp

Executive Story Editor—David Lloyd
Story Editor—Ken Estin
Associate Producer—Richard Sakai
Executive Consultant—James Brooks
Director—James Burrows
Film Editor—M. Pam Blumenthal
Art Director—Kenneth Reid
Director of Photography—Kenneth Peach
Unit Production Manager—Gregg Peters
Music—Bob James

"LOUIE'S RIVAL"

Episode #47

Synopsis: Louie is shattered when Zena Sherman tells him she wants to break off their relationship. Louie says, "Zena saw something in me that nobody else ever saw . . . that isn't there." Zena's new boyfriend is Dwight, the day bartender at Mario's, and Louie considers what he should do to him. Before Louie can act, though, he learns that Dwight already has plans to stop seeing Zena. Naturally, Louie is overjoyed to hear this—yet even after her relationship with Dwight ends, Zena says she's determined not to get involved with Louie again. But eventually Zena agrees, against her better judgment, to take Louie back.

Credits: James Burrows directed the script by Ken Estin. Rhea Perlman was the guest star as Zena Sherman, with Richard Minchenberg as Dwight and T. J. Castronova as Tommy.

"FATHERS OF THE BRIDE"

Episode #48

Synopsis: Louie reads a newspaper item to Alex which reports that Alex's daughter, Cathy, is going to marry a United Nations ambassador's son. (Alex has seen Cathy only once since he divorced Phyllis, her mother.) Alex is naturally angry that he has not received an invitation to the wedding, and he decides to attend anyway. Elaine insists on accompanying him to the lavish reception, where Alex confronts Phyllis. (We learn that Cathy wanted Alex to be there, but that Phyllis neglected to send out the invitation.) Alex and Phyllis begin bickering almost immediately. She frequently makes insulting remarks about Alex's choice of profession. "You would think that after eighteen years she could stop criticizing me," he says. But when they go off to a back room to settle their differences, they discover they still have an attraction for each other. At the end Cathy is pleased to see Alex and Phyllis hugging.

Credits: James Burrows directed the script by Barry Kemp. Louise Lasser was the guest star as Phyllis, with Talia Balsam portraying Cathy and Carlo Quintero portaying Carlo, Phyllis's second husband.

Viewers of *Taxi* can be sure that any episode which features Louise Lasser will be an especially lively one. She is terrific at handling the character of Phyllis, who's as anxiety-prone as anyone we ever see on the series. In "Fathers of the Bride," we get a sense of what Alex and Phyllis's marriage must have been like; the pairing of stolid Alex with volatile Phyllis must surely have produced its share of fireworks.

The writer of this episode, Barry Kemp, explains that "the production of 'Fathers of the Bride' was unusual because we needed a bigger set for the wedding reception than we normally used. So on the night we shot it, all three hundred people in the audience watched the first half of the episode performed on one stage, and then they were escorted by usher to another location for the last half, which was done on another stage nearby. . . . That was the only episode in which we used another stage."

"GOING HOME"

Episode #49

Synopsis: Jim's father, a millionaire, sends a private detective to New York in search of his son. The private detective explains that Jim's father is making out his will and wants to see all of his family again. We also learn that Reverend Jim's real last name is not Ignatowski, but Caldwell. Alex accompanies Jim to the Caldwell mansion in Boston, where Jim is reunited with his dad, his brother Tom, and his sister Lila. Mr. Caldwell stuns Alex by telling him that Jim once attended Harvard. Jim's dad wants to know what his son has been doing since college, and he's disgusted to learn that Jim has no ambitions whatsoever and that he has spent most of his life drifting aimlessly. Mr. Caldwell wants his son to shape up and get a decent job, but Jim has no interest in becoming more respectable. At the end it appears that although Jim and his father will never reconcile their differences, at least they're less hostile toward each other than before.

Credits: James Burrows directed the script by Glen Charles and Les Charles. Victor Buono was the guest star, in the part of Mr. Caldwell. Walter Olkewicz was Tom, Barbara Deutsch was Lila, Dick Yarmy was Spencer, the detective, and John Eames was the Caldwells' butler.

The viewer can't help but feel sorry for Jim's dad. After all, he gave his son every advantage, only to see Jim turn into an acidhead. Alex attempts, with little success, to assure Mr. Caldwell that Jim has been a good person and that Jim's life hasn't been a total waste. Alex says, "Mr. Caldwell, the only damage that Jim's ever done to anybody has been to himself." "He's done his share of that," responds Mr. Caldwell. Victor Buono skillfully communicates the disappointment that his character must feel.

"ELAINE'S STRANGE TRIANGLE"

Episode #50

Synopsis: Elaine's latest romance has just gone sour, so the cabbies try to cheer her up one day at Mario's. Kirk Muldaur, a handsome stranger, approaches Elaine and Tony at the bar. Soon, Tony and Alex are pressuring Kirk to ask Elaine out. After a few dates Elaine becomes quite interested in Kirk, but Kirk reveals to Tony that he is bisexual: "I honestly never meant to get involved with Elaine. . . . You remember the night I came up to you two at the bar, I said, 'Are you two together?' Well, she wasn't the one I was after." Kirk tells Tony that "your simplicity is engaging" and that "we'd be wonderful together." Tony convinces Alex to set Kirk straight (as it were) and to get Kirk to tell Elaine the truth. Alex meets Kirk in a gay bar, where Alex learns that Kirk has already told Elaine he's bisexual. Kirk says she now realizes that he just wants to be friends with her. At the end of the episode, Alex gets caught up in a dance at the gay bar.

Credits: James Burrows directed the script by David Lloyd. John David Carson was the guest star in the role of Kirk Muldaur.

James Burrows won an Emmy in 1981 for outstanding directing in a comedy series for his work on "Elaine's Strange Triangle." Burrows says, "I insisted we use only gay extras and bit players in the *Taxi* episode in the gay bar. Why? Because they look right and have the right behavior. I told my cast to be as real as possible. . . . We didn't have any 'wild' gays in it at all."

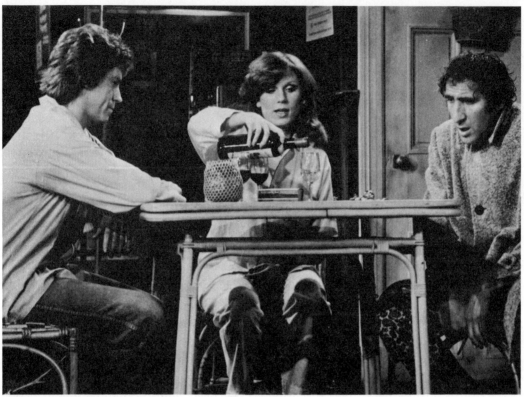

Alex shivers after running through a snowstorm over to Bobby's apartment in "Bobby's Roommate."

"BOBBY'S ROOMMATE"

Episode #51

Synopsis: Elaine's apartment building is going co-op, so she needs to find a new place to live. Since Bobby is leaving the city to tour for a month in *Under the Yum-Yum Tree*, he lets her stay in his apartment while she looks for a new home. She fixes up his apartment, which had been a mess, and all seems to be going well for both Bobby and Elaine. Bobby unexpectedly returns home a week later, though (he was fired for sleep- ing with the director's daughter), and he offers to let her stay on as his roommate. Elaine agrees, but Alex and Tony fear that Bobby will try to seduce her. Elaine is offended. "I really resent the implication that I would lose control," she says. Bobby is tempted to make a pass at Elaine, but he remains a gentleman. (In fact, Bobby becomes concerned that she will make a pass at *him*, and he calls Alex to come over.) Eventually, we are led to believe, Elaine finds a new apartment of her own.

Credits: James Burrows directed the script by Earl Pomerantz.

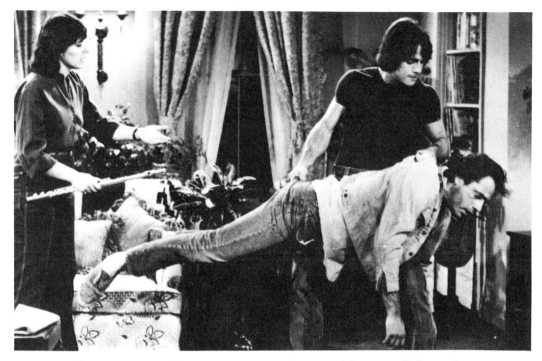

In "Tony's Sister and Jim," Tony tries to throw Reverend Jim out of Monica's apartment, literally.

A memorable exchange occurs in "Bobby's Roommate" when Elaine tells Alex what it was like being with Bobby. She says, "Bobby and I spoke about things I've never been comfortable talking about with a man before . . . Bobby's career, Bobby's hopes, Bobby's problems." "How did you manage to drag that out of him?" responds Alex.

"TONY'S SISTER AND JIM"

Episode #52

Synopsis: Tony's sister Monica arrives in New York. She's recently been divorced, and Tony is determined to fix her up with someone new. Tony wants her to become friendly with Alex, but she takes an immediate liking instead to Reverend Jim. Monica and Jim go out for dinner at an elegant French restaurant. He tells her, "It's been a long time since I had to be interesting." Jim and Monica hit it off well, though, and it's obvious that they are soon sleeping together. Tony is unhappy that his sister is involved with someone as flaky as Jim, and he begs Alex to take Monica out. When Alex declines, Tony says, "We're friends, huh? You don't think enough of me to go to bed with my sister." Next, Tony goes over to Monica's apartment and tries everything he can think of to break up Jim and

Monica's romance. Finally, Tony realizes he's being foolish and accepts that his sister's personal life is her own business.

Credits: James Burrows directed the script by Michael Leeson. Julie Kavner was the guest star as Monica. J. Alan Thomas appeared as Jeff and Andrew Block appeared as the maître d'.

An especially funny moment in this episode is when we see Jim's sly grin as he realizes that Monica really is interested in him. "When I think of you, I smile," she tells him. And he replies, "When I think of me, I smile, too."

"Tony's Sister and Jim" won an Emmy for Michael Leeson in 1981 for outstanding writing in a comedy series.

"CALL OF THE MILD"

Episode #53

Synopsis: Bobby travels to the mountains to make a commercial for Brickhauser beer. He gets such a taste for the outdoor life that he tries to talk the other guys into going back for a full week of roughing it in the woods. Alex, Tony, and Jim decide to go along with Bobby, while Elaine is skeptical about their adventure. When Elaine tells Bobby that their trip sounds "rough," he replies, "We want it rough, Elaine. We want to test our met-

tle. We want to stand face to face with nature in its most raw." But when the guys travel to a cabin in a remote spot, we see they are so used to life in the city that they are virtually helpless in the wilderness. They panic when they realize there is no refrigerator or telephone in the place. Furthermore, the man who guided them to the cabin will not be returning for a whole week. Tony asks, "What did the pioneers do in situations like these?" "They built cities and moved into them," responds Alex. The guys have a rifle, yet none of them seems able to bring himself to shoot an animal. Eventually, as starvation looms, a turkey walks into their cabin, and Alex musters the courage to kill it. Reverend Jim delivers a eulogy for the dead bird, and the guys have to overcome pangs of guilt before eating it.

Credits: James Burrows directed the script by Katherine Green. Harvey Vernon appeared as the guide.

Katherine Green, the writer of "Call of the Mild," says that "someone told me that this episode was as close as we ever got on *Taxi* to doing an *I Love Lucy* episode." That comment is definitely on the mark: what happens here is closer to the wacky, screwball situations of the fifties sitcoms than to the more realistic situations we usually see on *Taxi*. Because of this, "Call of the Mild," in spite of a few funny moments, doesn't really come off; we feel almost as if we've accidentally tuned in to the wrong series.

"THY BOSS'S WIFE"

Episode #54

Synopsis: Louie explains to the cabbies that whenever Mr. MacKenzie, the owner of the Sunshine Cab Company, and his wife have a big fight, Mrs. MacKenzie has an unusual way of getting her revenge. She always invites a cabbie, usually a young, handsome one, to her apartment for dinner—and other late-night activities. Then she reveals to her husband that she's gone to bed with one of his employees. Mr. MacKenzie goes through the roof, and afterwards the unfortunate cabbie is never seen around the garage again. When the boss and his wife get into a fight in this episode, she chooses Louie to be her new victim. "Why me?" he asks, sounding panic-stricken. Mrs. MacKenzie replies, "Because if my fooling around with someone halfway decent upsets my husband, then this'll kill him." Louie is terrified at the thought of what will happen to him if he goes to the MacKenzies', but he finally gives in to her offer. At the MacKenzie apartment, Louie resists her advances for a while, yet winds up in her bed. Just as Louie takes her into his lecherous arms, Mr. MacKenzie comes home. Mr. and Mrs. MacKenzie make up—while Louie cowers under the covers of their enormous bed.

Credits: James Burrows directed the script by Ken Estin. The guest stars were Stephen Elliott and Eileen Brennan as Mr. and Mrs. MacKenzie.

"LATKA'S COOKIES"

Episode #55

Synopsis: Latka's grandmother dies, and in her will she leaves him the recipe for some unusual cookies. Latka makes a batch of the cookies and hands them out to the cabbies. At first everyone finds them to be almost impossible to chew, but soon they can't seem to get enough of them. Latka wants to sell the cookies in stores, and he even tells Louie he's quitting work at the garage. "I don't need this job," says Latka. "I have the cookies, and I am going to be rich and famous, just like the Famous Amos, the chocolate-chip cookie tycoon." When Reverend Jim samples Latka's cookies, he notices something unusual. Jim identifies coca leaves, from which cocaine is made, in the cookies. Because of the cocaine, all of the cabbies are feeling a certain euphoria. Alex says, "I feel like I'm sort of happy.

Famous Amos himself makes an appearance in "Latka's Cookies."

I've got all this energy. And last night I had a little trouble falling asleep—so I wrote an opera." Finally, Alex informs Latka about the cocaine, the "secret ingredient" in his grandmother's recipe, and Latka realizes he won't be able to sell the cookies in stores. Alex and Latka are aware that they have become addicted to the drug, so they decide to go "cold turkey" and stop eating the cookies. They succeed in kicking the habit, and in a dream Latka imagines meeting Famous Amos, who advises him to "do whatever you can to become successful. Just get rich."

Credits: James Burrows directed the script by Glen Charles and Les Charles. Famous Amos was the guest star, playing himself, and J. Alan Thomas played Jeff.

The scene in which Reverend Jim samples Latka's cookies is highly entertaining. Jim sniffs the cookies and, with a connoisseur's knowledge, pronounces his verdict: there are coca leaves in the recipe. Furthermore, he identifies the coca leaves as being Peruvian, and he says that these particular leaves are "poignant, but not overbearing."

"THE TEN PERCENT SOLUTION"

Episode #56

Synopsis: Bobby is rejected for an acting role because he doesn't have the right look. "It's a handicap to be classically handsome," he says, adding that the "common look" is now in vogue. Since Tony has the kind of face that is supposed to be popular, he tries to convince Bobby that he could become a successful actor if Bobby were to manage him. Bobby agrees to represent him (even though Tony is hopelessly incompetent as an actor), and Bobby sends Tony's picture to dozens of casting directors around town. Tony gets an audition, and he's immediately hired for a small part in a movie. Nevertheless, he is fired by the director on his first day of work. Bobby says that this is a good thing: "It shows there's a powerful person who stands up for quality. . . . It means that acting and everything that the theater represents is still alive." "Just 'cause I got canned? Wow!" responds Tony, who is delighted with what Bobby has just said. "But I hope they don't expect me to bail 'em out every time," Tony adds.

Credits: James Burrows directed the script by Pat Allee. Sarina C. Grant appeared as a casting director. Jim Staskel and Ed. Weinberger appeared as producers of the movie.

Attentive viewers will note that Ed. Weinberger, one of the creators of *Taxi*, makes a brief appearance in "The Ten Percent Solution." Weinberger plays one of the producers who hire Tony for the part in the movie. (Weinberger's character is the one sitting on the right and wearing dark glasses.)

"ZEN AND THE ART OF CAB DRIVING"

Episode #57

Synopsis: Jim overhears some passengers in his cab talking about "dynamic perfectionism," and he becomes an enthusiastic follower of this self-help technique. Jim dumbfounds the other cab drivers when he says, "What a bunch of losers. . . . I'm talking about you, I'm talking about me, I'm talking about all of us. But I'm not gonna be a failure for long. I've found the secret: dynamic perfectionism." Surprising the other drivers even more, Jim sets out to become the ideal cabbie. "If you do everything as perfectly as you can, eventually you'll reach your goal," he explains. We see that he is putting his ideas into practice by driving almost twenty-four hours a day and by treating his passengers like royalty. Soon Jim is making much more money than anyone else in the history of the garage. One day Jim invites the other cabbies to his apartment, where he is to reveal his "secret goal" to them. The cabbies are disappointed when Jim shows them what he has been saving his money for: a gigantic home video center. At first, they tell him he's wasted his money, but then each of the cabbies finds something interesting to watch on one of Jim's TV sets.

Credits: Will McKenzie directed the script by Glen Charles and Les Charles. Nicholas Hormann and Michael Mann appeared as passengers in Reverend Jim's cab.

"ELAINE'S OLD FRIEND"

Episode #58

Synopsis: Elaine picks up a passenger in her cab one night who turns out to be an old high school friend, Mary Parker. Elaine and Mary were real competitors in school, and Elaine is intensely jealous when she discovers that Mary now owns a business and travels around the world with her boyfriend, Michael Edwards, an international lawyer. Elaine senses that Mary feels sorry for her, so she invents a story about having a boyfriend of her own, Bill Board, who's supposed to be a

In "Elaine's Old Friend," Alex pretends (?) to be in love with Elaine.

professor at Columbia. Mary wants the four of them to have dinner together, but Elaine tries to wriggle out of it. The next day Elaine is about to admit the truth to Mary over the phone. Then Alex comes to Elaine's aid and tells Mary that he is Elaine's guy and that he wants to have dinner with her and Michael. When all four of them meet at a restaurant, Alex plays the part of Elaine's boyfriend with great conviction, pretending to be absolutely crazy about her. Alex's act thoroughly convinces Mary and Michael; Mary even begins to feel jealous of Elaine's life. After leaving the restaurant, Elaine tries to get Alex to admit that he wasn't just acting—that he does feel a strong attraction for her. Alex won't admit this, yet we see that he does look upon Elaine as more than just a friend.

Credits: Jeff Chambers directed the script by Susan Jane Lindner and Nancy Lane. The guest star was Martha Smith, as Mary Parker. John Considine portrayed Michael Edwards and Myron Natwick portrayed the maître d'.

Judd Hirsch's performance in "Elaine's Old Friend" is especially good. When Alex tells Mary and Michael about how deeply he is in love with Elaine, it's clear that no one would doubt it. Alex explains that "when Elaine and I met, I became the perfectly happy man. And she's the most wonderful person I've ever met in my life. And every day makes me more certain of that fact." Alex's voice is filled with apparent sincerity when he delivers this speech. "Elaine's Old Friend" is definitely one of the funniest episodes of the series.

"THE COSTUME PARTY"

Episode #59

Synopsis: Bobby discovers a briefcase in the back seat of his cab, and it apparently belongs to someone with important connections in the theatrical world. From an entry in an appointment book they find in the briefcase, the cabbies learn of a costume party planned for the following Saturday. And from some initials and first names, they guess that the party is being thrown by Woody Allen. Bobby sees the party as an ideal opportunity to meet some high-powered theatrical producers, and the other cabbies are excited by the thought of meeting lots of celebrities. Bobby goes to the party as Cyrano de Bergerec; Elaine, as Scarlet O'Hara; Reverend Jim, as himself; and Tony, Alex, and Latka, as the Andrews Sisters. At the party, the cabbies think they're meeting Diane Keaton, Truman Capote, Al Pacino, and Henry Kissinger, but they soon discover that they've made a big mistake and that nobody there is actually famous. The cabbies leave the party almost immediately. Back in the garage, Tony, Alex, and Latka give their impression of the Andrews Sisters' performance of "Bei Mir Bist Du Schön."

Credits: James Burrows directed the script by David Lloyd. Hector Britter appeared as Gus Bates, Louis Guss appeared as Maxie, and Michael Klingher appeared as a policeman.

"OUT OF COMMISSION"

Episode #60

Synopsis: Tony is knocked out in the first round of his latest fight. Afterwards, the ring doctor examines him, and the doctor says he's concerned that Tony may have suffered some brain damage. Tony admits he has been knocked out fourteen times in his career, but he is adamant about wanting to continue boxing. The doctor takes Tony's case to the medical board, and the boxing commission revokes his license. Tony is crestfallen. He says to the other cabbies, "Without boxing, I'm just a cab driver." Tony is so distraught he tries to fight again under an assumed name. As Kid Rodriguez (!) Tony is scheduled for a bout at the Brooklyn Armory. Just before the fight, Alex, Bobby, and Jim come to Tony's dressing room and attempt to persuade him not to go through with it. Yet Tony does decide to fight, only to change his mind halfway through the bout and step out of the ring. Tony loses by default and hangs up his boxing gloves, apparently for good.

Credits: James Burrows directed the script by Sam Simon. Al Ruscio appeared as Dr. Webster, James F. Lennon was the ring announcer, Vince Delgado was the referee, Carmine Caridi was Lou-Lou, and Jessie Goins was Shotgun.

"Out of Commission" includes a particularly amusing exchange between Tony and Alex:

Tony: Without boxing, I'm just a cab driver. Just a lousy cab driver. . . . No offense, Alex.

Alex: That's alright, Tony. I'm not really a cab driver. I'm just waiting for something better to come along—like death.

"BOBBY AND THE CRITIC"

Episode #61

Synopsis: Bobby writes a scathing letter to the newspaper that publishes the reviews of John Bowman, a venomous theater critic who loves to say insulting things about actors. After Bobby finishes the letter, he realizes the damage to his career that would result if he mailed it to the newspaper. So he throws the letter into a wastebasket. Louie retrieves the letter, though, and sends it to the editor of the paper, who publishes it. Bobby fears the worst, but he receives scores of letters and calls praising him for his courage. And then Louie tells him, "A certain V.I.P. personality called the theater [where Bobby is appearing] to reserve a seat for tonight's performance." Louie joyfully reveals that the "V.I.P. personality" is John Bowman. After watching the play Bowman tells Bobby he was very impressed by his performance. Bowman shows Bobby a rave review of his acting in the play, and then Bowman proceeds to tear up the review. By not writing about the play at all, Bowman explains, he can keep Bobby in obscurity.

Credits: James Burrows directed the script by Barry Kemp. John Harkins was the guest star, in the role of John Bowman.

In "Bobby and the Critic" John Harkins adeptly portrays John Bowman, a critic who enjoys being malicious. (It can't be a coincidence that his name is similar to John Simon's.) Bowman shows Bobby a favorable review of his acting in a play, only to tear it up in his face and tell him, "A bad review could make you a hero. A good review could make you a star. No review at all will keep you anonymous, where you belong."

"LOUIE'S MOTHER"

Episode #62

Synopsis: Louie tells the cabbies that he's put his mother into a nursing home. And he admits that he knows nothing about the place. "You mean you didn't go there and check it out?" Tony asks him. Louie replies, "What the hell do I look like—Mike Wallace?" Louie decides to throw a party to celebrate his new-found freedom, now that his mother is out of his way. He invites Alex, who decides to attend in order to satisfy his sense of curiosity about what one of Louie's parties would be like. The only other guests at the party turn out to be three incredibly dull friends of Louie's: Lyle, Hughie, and Daytona Dave. A few days later Louie admits to the cabbies that he is lonely and misses his mother. He goes to the nursing home and asks his mother to come back: "Ma, when you're not there it's so quiet, I can hear the toilet running—I'm sorry for gettin' mushy." Louie's mom says to him, "If I come home, will you be nice to me?" "For a

In "Louie's Mother," Mrs. DePalma was played by Mrs. DeVito, Danny's mother.

while," replies Louie. Louie then escorts her out of the nursing home.

Credits: James Burrows directed the script by Katherine Green. Appearing as Mrs. DePalma was Julia DeVito.

The part of Louis DePalma's mother was played, appropriately enough, by Danny DeVito's mother, Julia. "Julia was around often on the set; she would come in from New York," recalls Ian Praiser. "And Jim [Brooks] very much wanted somebody who looked real. So it was decided to take a chance and use Julia. . . . In 'Louie's Mother' her part was really brief, so we weren't taking much of a risk in using her. We only see her for a moment as she walks down the corridor."

Taxi trivia buffs may be interested to know that when Mrs. DePalma speaks Italian, her voice is not Mrs. DeVito's, but that of a professional actress. (Mrs. DeVito's Italian was a bit rusty.)

"LOUIE BUMPS INTO AN OLD LADY"

Episode #63

Synopsis: Louie becomes interested in an attractive new cabbie, Janine. Louie offers to take Janine for a ride and give her some tips about being a taxi driver. But while he's driving Janine around, he gets into an accident: he runs into an old lady as she steps off a curb. He carries the injured woman, Edith Tremayne, into the Sunshine Garage. Next, Louie calls a doctor, rents a wheelchair, and buys roses for her. He hopes to avoid getting hit with a lawsuit, but she decides to sue the cab company in spite of all his efforts to soothe her. We soon learn, however, that the old lady is in cohoots with a crooked lawyer and that she has been in the habit of faking injuries from similar "accidents" in the past. When Louie discovers this, he's confident the case will be thrown out of court. What he doesn't

know is that this time she really *is* hurt. In court, Louie tells the judge about her history of fraud. Louie is so confident Edith is faking her injury that he pushes her (while she's still in her wheelchair) down a corridor in the courthouse. He is sure that she will get out of the wheelchair before she gets to the stairway. But since she really is unable to stand, she continues down the corridor until she reaches the steps—and then we hear the sound of the wheelchair crashing. (Fortunately for Louie, she isn't seriously hurt.) Needless to say, Louie loses his case. At the end Alex is leaving the garage to go bail Louie out of jail, and the other cabbies tell Alex to take his time getting there.

Credits: James Burrows directed the script by David Lloyd. Iris Korn was the guest star, portraying Edith Tremayne. Lane Brody appeared as Janine, Jay F. Riley appeared as a judge, and Sam De-Fazio and Joe Medalis appeared as lawyers.

"LATKA THE PLAYBOY"

Episode #64

Synopsis: Latka is such a bumbler that American women are not at all interested in him. So Latka starts studying *Playboy* magazine for tips on how to become a swinger. "I'm sick of you all calling me a cute little foreigner," he tells the cabbies. Latka takes a week's vacation and locks himself up in his apartment: he's deter-

Latka fails to make a good impression on a beautiful woman at Mario's in "Latka the Playboy."

minator, Robin Klein appeared as Karen, and T. J. Castronova appeared as Tommy.

Ian Praiser comments that "Andy Kaufman had expressed the fact that he was feeling a little restless in the part of Latka. And one way to keep Andy's interest up was to let him explore some of the other characters he did on stage. It was Jim Brooks's idea that Latka could become a multiple personality. . . . Vic Ferrari was the dark side of Latka. He could do all the things that Latka was afraid to do."

mined to transform himself into a new man. He loses his accent, begins wearing designer clothes—and turns into a fatuous boor. When Latka returns to the garage, he has become Vic Ferrari, a swinging bachelor. He now seems to know every line for seducing women. "Come on, walk with me, talk with me," he says to a pretty girl at Mario's. Soon it's obvious that Latka's transformation into Vic is not just an act—it's a full-blown case of multiple personality. The cabbies liked Latka, but they are extremely annoyed with Vic, and they tell him so to his face. Eventually, Vic comes to Alex and admits that he would like to change back into being Latka, but that he is unable to. "I went too far," Vic says. "I can't remember what I used to sound like." Yet in the end Alex does succeed in coaxing Vic back into becoming Latka again.

Credits: James Burrows directed the script by Glen Charles and Les Charles. George Wendt appeared as the exter-

"JIM THE PSYCHIC"

Episode #65

Synopsis: Reverend Jim, who often has "psychic" dreams, warns Alex that he will die in his apartment at 7:00 P.M. the following Thursday. Alex scoffs at Jim's premonition. "I happen to be a realistic person," Alex says. "I always have been and I always will be." But the other cabbies recall a number of unusual incidents when Jim's predictions have apparently come true. Tony says, "Maybe that guy *can* see into the future. He sure can't see into the present." Alex becomes increasingly distressed as several more of Jim's predictions prove to be correct. As Jim foretold, Alex (1) meets a beautiful blonde, (2) drinks a glass of water rapidly, (3) is mistaken for a girl, and (4) dances the cancan with a catcher's mask on. Still, Alex wants to confront the situation head-on and not be overcome by his fears. Louie comes to visit him just before the 7:00 P.M. deadline. Unlike Alex, Louie is superstitious and is convinced that Alex will die. Louie's fears prove contagious, and even Alex begins to have morbid thoughts. At seven o'clock precisely, there is a knock on the door—but it's only a little girl selling cookies. Louie, keyed up to the point of hysteria, screams—chasing the Girl Scout away.

Credits: James Burrows directed the script by Barry Kemp. Diane Peterson played Peggy and Kiva Dawson played the Girl Scout.

"The idea for this episode was contributed by Holly Holmberg Brooks" (the wife of James Brooks), recalls Barry Kemp, who wrote the script for "Jim the Psychic." Kemp explains, "It was one of those shows that were written in two days. We had received an order for two additional episodes right at the end of the season, and so we were really scrambling to come up with something fast. 'Jim the Psychic' was one of those two extra episodes added to the end of the season."

"FLEDGLING"

Episode #66

Synopsis: The Hazeltine Gallery, where Elaine works, has acquired a painting by a noted artist, Craig Eagen. Elaine is sent to his apartment to verify the authenticity of the painting. She asks Alex to accompany her, and he does. The artist has a reputation for being a recluse, and when Alex and Elaine come to his apartment, he refuses to let them in. Elaine charms Eagen into letting them get past his door, and it's immediately obvious that the artist has some serious problems. He admits he suffers from agoraphobia, a fear of the outside world. Elaine feels sorry for Eagen and wants to help him overcome his fears, but Alex says, "Elaine, this is out of your league. This man is damn near psychotic. . . . Why don't you get this man to a qualified psychiatrist?" Elaine won't listen to Alex; she insists that she can help Eagen to live a normal life. At first, she helps Eagen to step into his hallway (something he hasn't been able to do for years). Next, she brings him in her cab to the Sunshine Garage, where each of the other cabbies takes a turn at attempting to coax him to get out of the taxi. And not only does he finally succeed in taking a few steps outside of the cab, but he even dances around the garage with Elaine—while Louie hums "Stormy Weather."

Credits: James Burrows directed the script by Ken Estin. Paul Sand was the guest star, in the role of Craig Eagen.

Paul Sand does a fine job of portraying Craig Eagen, the incredibly reclusive artist shown in "Fledgling." Elaine tries her best to help him conquer some of his fears, though he seems to have enough problems to keep a whole staff of psychiatrists busy for years. "As I got older," Craig says, "I kept getting afraid of more and more things." Paul Sand is all tics as he skillfully conveys that his character is seriously disturbed yet mild-mannered and harmless. The Craig Eagen character is especially funny when he tries, with lots of difficulty, to smile. It looks as if it's been a long time since he has used those cheek muscles for smiling rather than frowning.

"ON THE JOB, PART I"

Episode #67

Synopsis: Louie informs the cabbies that the Sunshine Cab Company has gone bankrupt. He says, "It's your fault, all of you. You couldn't just drive and be happy you had jobs. No, everything had to be just so: the tires had to have treads, the brakes had to have linings. OK, prima donnas—you've got 'em. Now you don't have jobs." The cabbies realize they'll have to look for new jobs, and they agree to meet in a month's time at Mario's and share their experiences. And one month later they do get together to tell what has happened to each of them. Tony recounts that he took a job collecting gambling debts from people who owed money to a bookmaker. (Tony even had to collect from a priest who didn't have the money. He accepted a watch in lieu of the cash.) Elaine recounts that she worked as a secretary to a business executive; she convinced her boss to be more outspoken at the corporate board meetings, with the

Bobby has a new role to play in "On the Job."

result that both she and her boss were fired. Jim's job (which he was totally unsuited for) was that of a door-to-door salesman. Latka, we see, is now working as a busboy at Mario's.

Credits: James Burrows directed the script by Dennis Danziger and Ellen Sandler. Appearing in this episode were John O'Leary as the priest; Carmine Caridi as Cha-Cha, the bookmaker in Tony's segment; Bill Wiley as Mr. Givens, the business executive in Elaine's segment; John Petlock as the chairman of the board; Robert Balderson as Barrett; Alice Hirson as the woman in Jim's segment; and Robin Pearson Rose as Joanie.

"ON THE JOB, PART II"

Episode #68

Synopsis: The cabbies continue to talk about the jobs they've worked at since the cab company went broke. Louie recounts that he briefly was one of the most successful (and, we might add, detestable) stockbrokers on Wall Street; he conned a brokerage firm into hiring him. Louie devised a number of ethically dubious methods of drumming up more business, and he was successful at increasing the firm's profits. Still, he was fired anyway, because his coworkers found his boorish manners to be repulsive. Bobby says that his job involved entertaining at children's parties. On one occasion he dressed up as the Easter Bunny to amuse the little friends of the children of an important movie director. To impress the director, Bobby (while still wearing his Easter Bunny outfit) performed a scene from the play *Whose Life Is It Anyway?* Alex's job was that of a night watchman in an office building. Alex recounts that after a while he began to go crazy with boredom, talking to himself and acting silly in front of the TV monitors. At the end of the episode Louie announces that a new owner has been found for the Sunshine Cab Company. Very reluctantly, Alex, Tony, Elaine, Bobby, and Jim decide to go back to work as taxi drivers.

Credits: James Burrows directed the script by Dennis Danziger and Ellen Sandler. Appearing in this episode were Claire Malis, as Cynthia; Michael McGuire, as Mr. Gray; and Al Lewis, as a security guard.

The writers made it clear in this episode that the cabbies' pipe dreams aren't ever likely to come true. When they learn that the Sunshine Cab Company is back in business, Alex and Tony have this to say:

Alex: So cab driving is a stinky, lousy job that has no comforts and no dignity and no future. But on the other hand. . . . Would anyone like to help me out with the other hand?
Tony: On the other hand we stink at everything else?

And so the cabbies realize that they have nothing better to do than to go back to the Sunshine Garage.

One other thing about "On the Job": Bobby's segment is an especially memorable one. As he begins to do his bit from *Whose Life Is It Anyway?* he attempts to work it into his entertainment for the children. "That's right, boys and girls," Bobby says, "the Easter Bunny is also a serious artist."

FOURTH-SEASON CREDITS

Alex Rieger—Judd Hirsch
Elaine Nardo—Marilu Henner
Louie DePalma—Danny DeVito
Tony Banta—Tony Danza
Jim Ignatowski—Christopher Lloyd
Latka Gravas—Andy Kaufman

Executive Producers—James Brooks, Stan Daniels, and Ed. Weinberger

121

Producers—Ken Estin, Howard Gewirtz, and Ian Praiser
Coproducer—Richard Sakai
Executive Script Consultant—David Lloyd
Executive Story Editor—Sam Simon
Associate Producer—Greg Nierman
Executive Consultants—Glen Charles and Les Charles
Executive Creative Consultant—James Brooks
Film Editor—M. Pam Blumenthal
Art Director—Tommy Goetz
Director of Photography—Kenneth Peach
Unit Production Manager—Gregg Peters
Music—Bob James

"VIENNA WAITS"

Episode #69

Synopsis: Elaine's ex-husband Vince shows up unexpectedly and agrees to look after Jason and Jennifer for four weeks. Elaine seizes the opportunity to take a European vacation. She asks Alex to accompany her. At first, he's hesitant about going. Elaine says, "OK, Alex, you're going to miss what could be the best time of your fearful, suspicious little life." Alex is persuaded by Elaine to come along, but only on the condition that he will be free to go out with other women while he and Elaine are on their vacation. So Alex and Elaine are off to tour Europe, envisioning romantic evenings in Vienna, London, and Athens. What really happens when they get to Europe, however, is that Elaine finds eager suitors everywhere, while Alex bombs out time and time again. Alex becomes depressed about being alone in the evenings. The only good moments of the trip for Alex are the times when he and Elaine write postcards to send home. On their last evening in Europe, Elaine realizes what Alex has been going through, and she tells him, "Alex, we've known each other for four years now. . . . Maybe our friendship is strong enough to survive one night of love." And so Elaine and Alex go off to spend the night together.

Credits: Howard Storm directed the script by Ken Estin. Warwick Sims portrayed James, Gary Phillips portrayed Todd, Cassandra Gava portrayed Desiree, and Reuven Bar-Yotam portrayed Oumas.

The chemistry between Alex and Elaine is especially appealing in this episode. The first scene, in which Elaine tries to get Alex to go to Europe with her, is very enjoyable. While Elaine impulsively decides to just pick up and leave the country for four weeks, Alex is a much more cautious person. Judd Hirsch conveys a lot of what Alex feels in scenes like these just by the way he carries himself. Alex has the sagging shoulders of a man who expects nothing ever to go right.

Another interesting point about "Vienna Waits" is that it was the first episode of *Taxi* in which Jeff Conaway didn't appear.

"MR. PERSONALITIES"

Episode #70

Synopsis: Latka's habit of changing personalities prompts Elaine to make an appointment for him with her psychiatrist, Dr. Jeffries. Alex convinces Latka to go see the psychiatrist. "There's nothing to be afraid of," explains Alex. "You have a stomach-ache, you go to a doctor, right? You have a toothache, you go to a dentist. You have primary and secondary ego diffusion, you go to a psychiatrist." At Dr. Jeffries's office, Latka assumes a whole series of different personalities—including an impersonation of Alex. Back at the Sunshine Garage, Latka continues playing the part of Alex; he gives out advice to the other cabbies, just as the real Alex usually does. (What's worse, the other cabbies seem to like the "new" Alex better than the old one.) Both Alex and Latka then go back to see the psychiatrist. During their session together, Latka continues to assume the personality of Alex. Latka (still playing Alex) says to the psychiatrist, "I'm starting to realize my love for life is unrequited. . . . So I was really down, until suddenly it came to me: the exact thing I should do to put my life in order." At this point, Alex is desperately anxious to hear what Latka has to say, and then—just at the moment when he is about to give the solution to all of Alex's problems—Latka turns back into his old self.

Credits: Howard Storm directed the script by Ian Praiser and Howard Gewirtz. Barry Nelson was the guest star, in the role of Dr. Jeffries. Bernadette Birkett portrayed Doris Marie Winslow, Wendy Goldman portrayed Lynn, and T. J. Castronova portrayed Tommy.

The best scene in this episode is the one in which Latka (impersonating Alex) talks to the psychiatrist about some of Alex's problems. His comments are as accurate as anything the real Alex ever says about himself. "I've got a mediocre job," says Latka (as Alex). "But it doesn't stimulate me. I like my friends, but the nature of the relationship seems to be that I'm some kind of authority figure. I listen to their problems, and I'm not supposed to have any. I take pride in accepting things the way they are, but I just realized that maybe that's an excuse for not having any ambition." While Latka's talking, Alex keeps nodding his head—he recognizes the truth of what Latka is saying about him. And when Latka changes back to normal, Alex's disappointment is very entertaining.

"JIM JOINS THE NETWORK"

Episode #71

Synopsis: Reverend Jim picks up some important television executives in his cab; he overhears one executive, Janine, tell the other, Mitch, that if he doesn't come up with a hit series soon, he will be fired. Janine gets out of the cab, and as Jim drives Mitch to his destination Jim asks Mitch some questions about the TV world. "I always wondered how the networks decide what shows to put on," says

Elaine tries to persuade Louie not to kill a mouse that has taken up residence in the garage in "Jim Joins the Network."

Jim. According to Mitch, "It's a lot of complex variables. We look at sex, education, income—it's very scientific." The TV programmers may have their "scientific" techniques, but Jim has his own psychic hunches about the future that often prove to be uncannily accurate. Mitch tells Jim about two shows that he's going to be putting on the air, and Jim gives him his hunches about which will do well in the ratings. Mitch listens to what Jim says, although we see he doesn't take him at all seriously. Yet when the ratings come out, Jim is proven correct. Mitch then goes to the Sunshine Garage and asks Jim for help in making some programming decisions. Mitch brings Jim to his office, in the guise of a shoeshine boy (Mitch doesn't want anyone to know what Jim is really doing there), and puts Jim's psychic powers to work. Jim's hunches continue to be accurate, and Mitch becomes the fair-haired boy with his superiors. When Alex learns that Jim isn't being paid for his suggestions, he gets angry with Jim and convinces him to demand to be treated with dignity. Eventually, Mitch offers to pay Jim, but he refuses the money; Jim says he won't accept any financial gain for the use of his gifts.

Credits: Noam Pitlik directed the script

by David Lloyd. The guest star was Martin Short, as Mitch, and Melendy Britt appeared as Janine.

Martin Short, best known for his appearances on *SCTV,* brings a droll touch to the character he plays in "Jim Joins the Network." We see how disappointed in himself Mitch is for having to depend on someone as flaky as Jim to make his important decisions for him. "I can't believe I'm letting a cab driver from off the street do my job for me," says Mitch. Reverend Jim replies, "Don't feel bad—if you *could* do your job, you would." Jim then pats Mitch on the shoulder, in a gesture of reassurance. But Mitch's expression clearly shows that he is even more distressed than before.

"LOUIE'S FLING"

Episode #72

Synopsis: Emily, a good friend of Zena's, has just been dumped by a guy. Louie comes over to watch the Miss Universe Pageant on TV at Zena's apartment, and he's annoyed to find that Emily is there and that she is crying helplessly. Emily is so upset she's been taking lots of pills. "I probably shouldn't drink," says Emily. "I'm taking some medication. I've had a mild sedative from my doctor. And one from my mother. And, oh yeah, the super gave me one." Zena wants to comfort her friend, and she asks Louie to escort Emily home. Louie reluctantly calls Alex, who drives them in his cab to Em-

ily's place. Louie walks Emily to her door, and once inside he sees a chance to make a pass at her—and he winds up sleeping with Emily. As Louie later describes the scene to the cabbies, "There she was—dejected, desperate, and stoned. Everything I could hope for in a woman." Louie brags about having two girlfriends at the same time, but Elaine threatens to let Zena know what has happened. Realizing that he can't keep his fling with Emily a secret, he decides to confess to Zena. When Louie tells Zena he plans to go on seeing both her and Emily, Zena responds by informing Louie that she never wants to talk to him again. Next, Louie is rejected by Emily. She sums up her feelings about him by saying, "In the light of day, you're gross and disgusting." After having been dumped by both girls, Louie comes back to the garage and begs Alex for advice on how to salvage his relationship with Zena. Alex sensibly recommends that Louie should tell Zena he's giving up Emily for her—and that Louie should humbly beg for forgiveness. Louie goes off to plead with Zena.

Credits: James Burrows directed the script by Sam Simon. The guest stars were Rhea Perlman, as Zena, and Andrea Marcovicci, as Emily.

"LIKE FATHER, LIKE SON"

Episode #73

Synopsis: Alex's father, Joe, calls the cab company and tells Alex that he wants them to be friends. (They have spoken together on only one other occasion in the past twenty years: when Alex came to visit Joe in a hospital.) Alex and his father have dinner at Mario's. They meet a terrific woman, Karen, there; Joe encourages Alex to ask her out. Alex and Karen then make a date. But after Alex leaves, Joe can't resist his impulse to ask Karen out himself—Joe is a real ladies' man. Louie has observed the whole incident at Mario's, and he gets a kick out of it. "Rieger's on thin ice, and I'm a blowtorch," he tells Tommy, the bartender at Mario's. Soon both Alex and Joe are going out with Karen regularly. Karen's alternating dates with father and son continue until Louie can contain his glee no longer and blurts out the news to Alex. "She's two-timin' you with your old man," Louie says. Alex goes to Joe's apartment to tell him off—yet they wind up having dinner together on fairly friendly terms. After all these years of bad feelings between them, Alex realizes that it's pointless for him to hold a grudge against Joe.

Credits: James Burrows directed the script by David Lloyd. The guest star was Jack Gilford, as Joe, while Barbara Babcock played Karen and T. J. Castronova played Tommy.

"LOUIE'S MOM REMARRIES"

Episode #74

Synopsis: Louie relates to the cabbies that his mother has plans to marry a Jap-

anese man, Itsumi Fujimoto, whom she has recently met. Louie is adamant about not giving his blessing to the marriage, even though Alex, Elaine, and Tony explain that his mother needs companionship. Louie's mom, Gabriela De-Palma, comes to the garage and asks Louie to meet Mr. Fujimoto. Louie has a talk with the Japanese man, yet he still insists to his mother, "I won't be your son anymore if you marry him." Eventually, Alex persuades Louie to attend the wedding, and Louie does give his blessing to his mother's marriage. The wedding ceremony is presented in the traditional Japanese style.

Credits: James Burrows directed the script by Earl Pomerantz, Julia DeVito was the guest star as Gabriela DePalma, and Jerry Fujimoto portrayed Itsumi Fujimoto.

"We wanted to bring the character of Louie's mother back," explains Ian Praiser, one of the producers of *Taxi* at the time this episode was filmed, "and the question was: 'Can somebody that old handle it?' . . . But Danny's mother was just great. She never appeared nervous. Her comments on the set were terrifically funny. And she was never a problem: she took her changes well. You had to sort of hold her hand a little more than with the average person, but what a trooper she was for her to be able to do it as easily as she did. After all, she had had no experience as an actress before her first appearance on the show."

Howard Gewirtz and Ian Praiser, two producers of *Taxi*, are shown in this scene from "Of Mice and Tony." Praiser is on the far right, while Gewirtz is third from the right. *(Courtesy of Ian Praiser)*

"OF MICE AND TONY"

Episode #75

Synopsis: Tony tells Alex, "I finally found something in my life to take the place of boxing—managing. I found this great heavyweight, down at my gym. Alex, I think this guy could go all the way." Tony has lunch with the young heavyweight, Terry Carter, at Mario's, and he convinces Terry to let him be his manager. Meanwhile, Louie is on a losing streak with Alex; they've been betting on football games and Louie owes Alex twenty-six hundred dollars. When Louie hears that Tony is now a boxing manager, Louie sees a chance for a "sure thing" and bets double or nothing against Tony's heavyweight. Before the fight Tony is optimistic: "All my life I had this feeling that it wasn't supposed to happen for me. You know, like I was jinxed. Like I had an albacore around my neck. But ever since Terry signed up with me, that feelin' has been gone." Terry wins his fight, but afterwards a Dr. Frazier, who's fronting for a syndicate, comes to Terry's dressing room and offers to buy his contract. Since they can afford to give him much better opportunities than Tony could, Terry gives in to them. (Tony thinks the "syndicate" is part of organized crime, when actually they're a group of doctors.) At the end, Tony and Alex are disappointed about Terry's decision, but pleased that they've come out ahead financially. Alex has won fifty-two hundred dollars from Louie, and Tony has been paid five thousand dollars by the syndicate for Terry's contract. They go to Mario's to celebrate.

Credits: James Burrows directed the script by Glen Charles and Les Charles. The guest star, in the role of Terry Carter, was Ernie Hudson. John Christy Ewing appeared as Dr. Frazier, Jimmy Lennon was the ring announcer, Gene LeBell was the referee, Howard Gewirtz was Dr. Stokely, and Ian Praiser was Dr. Hardon.

Two producers of *Taxi*, Howard Gewirtz and Ian Praiser, have small parts in "Of Mice and Tony." They portray doctors from the "syndicate." Gewirtz is Dr. Stokely and Praiser is Dr. Hardon, who says to Tony, "That was quite a knockout. I've never seen anybody go out like that—and I'm an anesthesiologist." Praiser remembers, "I was so nervous about it during the dress rehearsal that I said 'gynecologist' instead of 'anesthesiologist.' The actors wouldn't let up on me; they kept ragging me. When it came time to say the line on camera, everybody was looking at me to see if I was going to say 'gynecologist' and hoping I would. But actually I acquitted myself quite

well. . . . It was Jim's [Brooks] idea to use us in this episode. We all look Jewish enough to be Jewish syndicate doctors from New Rochelle."

"NINA LOVES ALEX"

Episode #76

Synopsis: Nina, an attractive black girl, joins the Sunshine Cab Company. She's a very energetic and positive-thinking person. Nina is immediately attracted to Alex, and soon she begins making suggestions about getting together with him. Alex says "no" to all of her overtures. Nina keeps after him, though, giving him flowers and leaving romantic notes for him. Alex becomes increasingly irritated as Nina continues to pursue him. Alex insists to Elaine that he's not at all interested in Nina. He says, "Going past the difference in our age and going past the difference in our race and going past the difference in our attitudes and interests and metabolism, and the fact that she's a crazy little actress who likes to sing in her cab and wears ditzy clothes and has a view of the world shared only by Jiminy Cricket—going past all that and getting down to the real heart of the matter, I don't like her." Nina invites herself to Alex's apartment one night when she's expecting to find out about an audition she's given recently. Alex has a "get lost" speech all ready to give her. Yet when the usually optimistic Nina is dejected because she learns she didn't get the part, Alex tries to comfort her. He also tells her

Relaxing before filming an episode from the 1981–82 season were (left to right) Ken Estin, producer; Nat Bernstein, production assistant; Howard Gewirtz, producer; Sam Simon, executive story editor; Leslie Maier, production secretary; Ian Praiser, producer; and Les and Glen Charles, producers. *(Courtesy of Ian Praiser)*

he's sorry that he doesn't think they should get involved romantically. "Look, Nina, the basic problem with us is that you're looking for magic . . . and I'm a no-magic man." At the end Nina asks Alex to kiss her good night. He does, and finds himself unexpectedly attracted to Nina. But as soon as she sees he's really interested in her, she quickly gets up and leaves Alex's apartment.

Credits: Joan Darling directed the script by David Lloyd. Charlaine Woodard was the guest star as Nina.

Only a terribly dull-witted person would be able to watch "Nina Loves

Alex" without at least raising a smile. Charlaine Woodard's delightful performance is full of pep, and Judd Hirsch plays up the sour side of Alex Rieger. Alex gets increasingly irritated with Nina because she's too happy-go-lucky for his tastes. He tells Elaine, "I've got a problem. How do you stop somebody from brightening up your life?" And when Elaine says to Alex, "Come on, big fella, I know you don't go on like this about anything unless you have a connection," we're treated to a display of Hirsch's expert comic timing. Alex replies, trying to avoid giving away his interest in Nina, "Then I just won't go on about it. I have absolutely no need to go on about it. And what's more, the last thing I need in my life is a born-again cheerleader."

Another good point about Hirsch's performance here is that Alex doesn't deliver his lines as if he knew they were witty—instead, he just slips them in. Notice how he responds when Nina says, "This is my first night [as a taxi driver], and I'm lookin' forward to it, too. It should be exciting: couples going to the movies, kids on their first dates, anniversaries. Lots of happy people." Alex, who looks at cab driving as a dull routine, says, "I see you're planning on driving in the borough of Oz."

"LOUIE GOES TOO FAR"

Episode #77

Synopsis: Louie sinks (if it's possible for Louie to become even more sleazy

than before) to spying on Elaine in the ladies' room. Elaine finds out and becomes enraged. She brings a leader from the National Organization for Women to the garage to threaten a lawsuit, and they succeed in getting Mr. Ratledge, the current owner of the Sunshine Cab Company, to fire Louie. Now fully realizing the serious predicament he's in, Louie goes to Elaine's apartment to beg for forgiveness. Louie grovels pathetically, yet Elaine says she can't forgive him unless he is able to understand what was wrong with what he did. Louie desperately tries to convince her that he really does understand: "Object, I was treatin' you like a sexual object. . . . Thank God I watched that Donahue show about broads." But Elaine won't accept this as an explanation. Finally, he wins her forgiveness by telling her a poignant story about the embarrassment he feels when he needs to buy new clothes. To find things that fit him, he must go to the boys' departments of clothing stores, where the kids laugh at him. Elaine is touched, and she tries to comfort Louie by hugging him. He shows he is still the same old Louie by making a grab at her.

Credits: Michael Lessac directed the script by Daniel Kallis. Noni White appeared as Andrea Stewart, the official from NOW, and Allen Williams appeared as Robert, Elaine's date.

The story that Louie tells about going to the boys' departments to buy new clothes comes from Danny DeVito's own experiences. Just as in "Louie Goes Too Far," DeVito had once been told, "You're lucky. At least you won't outgrow it in six months." This scene is as close as Louie ever comes to revealing himself, and characteristically he undercuts it by pinching Elaine on the rear when he hugs her after finishing his story.

"I WANNA BE AROUND"

Episode #78

Synopsis: Louie is preparing for the end of the world. (A recent show by Phil Donahue has convinced him that doomsday is near.) He has turned the tool room at the garage into a survival shelter, with supplies of dehydrated food. "This must have cost you a fortune," Elaine says to him, after she sees all of his elaborate preparations. Louie replies, "What good is money in the bank, Nardo, when you're a radioactive pretzel?" Louie has even picked three people—Elaine, Jeff, and Tony—to form a "survival squad" with him (though Elaine refuses to have anything to do with his scheme). Alex tells Louie, "I don't think that that little group of yours would last two days in there." Louie accepts the challenge and decides to practice what he'll do when the world ends: he plans to spend two days in the shelter with Tony and Jeff. But, unbeknownst to Louie, Reverend Jim has slipped into the shelter and is hiding in a radioactive suit. Louie orders Tony to throw Jim out of their sanctuary, but nobody, not even Louie, has the heart to banish Jim. Finally, Louie gives up on his scheme.
Credits: James Burrows directed the script by Glen Charles and Les Charles.

The guest star was J. Alan Thomas as Jeff.

"I Wanna Be Around" is undoubtedly a candidate for the dubious honor of being the worst episode of the series. The basic situation is truly bizarre, to say the least. And to top it off, the writers made a big mistake in showing us Louie's "tender" side at the end of the episode. "I was done in by a soft heart," Louie tells Alex. "I couldn't throw Ignatowski out of there. When it came right down to it, I was soft. I'm a loser, like you." Who could believe that Louie would ever admit such a thing? Apparently, in this particular episode, the writers forgot that the whole secret of Louie's character is that, underneath his tough exterior, Louie most definitely does *not* have a heart of gold.

"BOBBY DOESN'T LIVE HERE ANYMORE"

Episode #79

Synopsis: The cabbies decorate the Sunshine Garage with banners in anticipation of Bobby's visit from Hollywood. Bobby has been gone from New York for six months, and he is waiting to find out if he has landed a part in a pilot, entitled *Boise*, for a TV series. (Bobby's character is the oldest son of a family from Idaho.) He gets a call from his agent and learns that the network has bought the pilot. Still, Louie is confident that the pilot will never become a regular series; he delivers a succession of put-downs about Bobby's acting abilities. Bobby is excited about the good news concerning *Boise,* and he takes a suite at the Plaza Hotel for a lavish party. But during the celebration, Bobby gets another call from his agent. Bobby learns that although the network has bought the series, the producers have decided to recast his part. Bobby is heartbroken when he tells the cabbies, "They said I wasn't sexy enough." Bobby feels dejected, yet he decides to go back to California and continue to try his luck at acting for television.

Credits: James Burrows directed the script by Glen Charles and Les Charles. Jeff Conaway was the guest star as Bobby Wheeler.

This episode is the last one in which the character of Bobby Wheeler makes an appearance on *Taxi.*

"TONY'S LADY"

Episode #80

Synopsis: Tony announces to the other cabbies that he has taken a second job, as a chauffeur to a wealthy family. One of the members of the family is Christina, a refined young lady whom Tony considers to be as stunning as any girl he's ever met. At first, Tony is terribly nervous while driving her, but she puts him at his ease; he then entertains her with stories about his boxing career. For instance, he describes his biggest fight: "I once fought

Ron Thomas. In his prime he was one of the best middleweights of all time. By the time I fought him he was forty-three. His reflexes were off, his timing was bad, his punches were weak. With a couple of breaks, I might've beaten him." Tony wants to ask Christina out, but he's afraid she's too far above him and looks at him as just the hired help. Alex, Elaine, and Jim convince him to make his move, and Tony decides he will ask her for a date. Just before he's able to get out the words to Christina, though, another guy asks her to marry him; she says "yes" and Tony is left feeling depressed.

Credits: Michael Zinberg directed the script by Ken Estin. The guest star was Rebecca Holden, playing Christina. John Calvin appeared as Doug and Joel Brooks appeared as Mr. Dwyer.

Tony Banta's infatuation with Christina is quite touching. Tony Danza is especially convincing when his character says, "I want her *so* bad, but she's out of my league. . . . I'm not goin' after no more pipe dreams. I can't take that again. I was a boxer, and I spent thirteen years of my life chasin' something I never got."

"SIMKA RETURNS"

Episode #81

Synopsis: Simka Dahblitz returns to New York, and she and Latka rekindle their interest in each other. The only difficulty is that Latka is still suffering from his multiple-personality problem. Simka goes to Latka's apartment for dinner, and the evening seems to be progressing nicely until Latka has one of his changes of personality. He becomes Vic Ferrari, who also finds himself attracted to Simka. Vic turns on his charm, and Simka succumbs to his seduction techniques. The next day Simka confesses to Latka. He is naturally disturbed by what has happened. "You have shamed me," Latka tells her. "You have degraded yourself, disgraced your family, cheapened your people, and blemished your planet." And soon Latka discovers that Simka and Vic have plans to fly off to Bermuda for a vacation together. Latka begs Simka not to go with Vic, and then we see that she really does prefer Latka to his alter ego. Even when he turns into Vic again briefly, Simka insists she wants Latka. At the end Latka turns back into his old self.

Credits: Michael Zinberg directed the script by Howard Gewirtz and Ian Praiser. The guest star, portraying Simka Dahblitz, was Carol Kane.

Carol Kane won an Emmy in 1982 for being the outstanding leading actress in an episode of a comedy series for her performance in "Simka Returns." Ian Praiser comments that "Carol Kane works from under the skin of her characters, from the inside out. I remember she was very anxious about how she would do in this episode until she had a clearer understanding of what her character was all about: she needed to know that Simka was a plucky girl from the home country."

"JIM AND THE KID"

Episode #82

Synopsis: Tony picks up Terry, a ten-year-old runaway, in his cab and drives him back to the garage. The boy takes a special liking to Reverend Jim, and Terry even goes to Jim's apartment and begs to be allowed to stay there. Good-hearted Jim agrees after hearing Terry's "horror" stories about how his parents force him to keep his room clean. Terry doesn't want to go to school, but Jim tells him, "School is very important. If I had dropped out of grammar school, I wouldn't have been able to drop out of college." Jim and the boy hit it off so well that Jim wants to adopt him. Meanwhile, Terry's parents are desperately searching for their son. Alex and Elaine find this out, and they convince Jim that Terry's place is with his parents. (Jim resists until he hears about Terry's lonely puppy.) At the end Terry's parents come to Jim's apartment and pick up their son.

Credits: Michael Zinberg directed the script by David Lloyd. Tony LaTorre was the guest star as Terry, with Mark Harrison and Rebecca Clemons appearing as Mr. and Mrs. Booth.

"TAKE MY EX-WIFE, PLEASE"

Episode #83

Synopsis: Alex goes on a double date with Tony and a set of great-looking twins, Randi and Candi. They are all at a

French restaurant when Alex spots his ex-wife Phyllis, who's recently been divorced by her latest husband. She wants to get back together with Alex, but he tells her, "We're simply just not involved in each other's lives anymore." When Louie hears about Phyllis's situation, he is pleased. "Personally, I love divorced women," Louie says. "I love women who have just broken up with guys. I live on the rebound. I love the rebound. I *am* the rebound." Phyllis comes to the garage, and Louie manages to get a date with her. Louie tells Alex about his date with Phyllis, and Alex is upset. "I don't want you to do that, Louie," Alex says. "Now she's weak, she's vulnerable, and she might mistake you for a human being." Alex goes to Phyllis's hotel room to warn her about Louie. (When Louie arrives, Alex has to hide in the bathroom.) Louie comes into Phyllis's room—and almost immediately flops into her bed. She screams, and Alex comes to her rescue. Phyllis and Alex go out to dinner together, but it still seems likely that they won't be getting romantically involved again.

Credits: Noam Pitlik directed the script by Ian Praiser and Howard Gewirtz. Louise Lasser was the guest star as Phyllis, with Randi and Candi Brough appearing as Randi and Candi Moratta.

One of the writers of this episode, Ian Praiser, remembers, "We rode a real roller coaster with Louise Lasser that week, though it turned out great in the end. . . . Louise is a very unusual actress in her working methods. She's very instinctive and doesn't know from moment to moment whether or not she's as good

as we all know she is. So she panics. No matter how good we told her she was, Louise was convinced that she was giving a terrible performance. Right until the cameras rolled, we were still wondering if she would come through for us. She works on the edge."

This is an excellent episode—the collision of Phyllis, the ultimate neurotic, with Louie, the ultimate lecher, makes for some hilarious moments, such as Louie's brief "date" with Phyllis. Apparently, Louie's idea of romancing a woman is to jump right into her bed at the beginning of their first date and say, "Have I got an evening planned for us. I already called room service, and they are sending up champagne, canapés—and oxygen."

"THE UNKINDEST CUT"

Episode #84

Synopsis: Elaine explains to the other cabbies that she's going to be attending the opening of a Japanese costume show at the Met. She'll be sitting next to a guy she is especially eager to impress, so she wants to look as good as she possibly can for the evening. She decides to make an appointment with Vincenzo Senaca, one of the most famous hair stylists in the city. (He charges $225 for a haircut.) Vincenzo says to Elaine, "Just as Michelangelo discovered the beauty of David in a slab of marble, I shall find in that head of hair your perfect hair style." But her haircut winds up looking ghastly—so weird that Elaine screams when she looks into the mirror. She is crying as she pays, and she runs out of the salon. Vincenzo calls after her, "I guess I just can't do cab drivers." The other cabbies are stunned at the sight of Elaine's haircut, and Alex insists she go back to the salon and demand restitution. Elaine tells Vincenzo off, and Louie comes along and dumps hair-setting solution on Vincenzo's head.

Credits: Noam Pitlik directed the script by Sam Simon, from a story by Barbara Duncan and Holly Holmberg Brooks. Ted Danson was the guest star as Vincenzo Senaca. Also appearing were Gela Jacobson as the receptionist, Sam Scarber as the video installer, J. Alan Thomas as Jeff, and Karen Anders as the drunk woman.

The idea for this episode was contributed by Holly Holmberg Brooks, the wife of James Brooks. Like Elaine in "The Unkindest Cut," Holly had been through the experience of becoming furious with a hairdresser who had given her a terrible, silly-looking haircut, not at all what she had wanted—and who had overcharged her, to boot.

Ted Danson, who does a terrific job as Vincenzo Senaca, was first approached to play the lead in *Cheers* during the week he made this episode of *Taxi*. Danson was told about the role of Sam Malone by James Burrows, the director of seventy-six episodes of *Taxi* and one of the creators of *Cheers*.

"TONY'S COMEBACK"

Episode #85

Synopsis: Lucius Franklin, a pro football player who's been cut by one NFL team and who's waiting to try out for another, joins the Sunshine Cab Company. Lucius works out to keep in shape, and he invites Tony to join him at the gym. We learn that Lucius is one of those positive-thinking types of people who say that if a person believes in himself, he can be anything he wants to be. With his enthusiasm Lucius is able to instill a new sense of confidence in Tony. Lucius even gets Tony to take a physical to see if he has recovered from his concussion. Tony then appeals to the boxing commission and succeeds in getting his boxing license back. Lucius soon leaves the garage to join the Miami Dolphins, and Tony quickly loses most of his motivation to work hard. He recruits Alex to take Lucius's place as his manager, but Alex has trouble being tough enough with Tony to force him to do all his exercises. Yet Tony does manage to set up a bout. At first it seems that Tony is sure to lose, but Lucius returns to New York for the fight and urges him on. To his own (and the other cabbies') surprise, Tony wins convincingly.

Credits: Michael Lessac directed the script by Sam Simon. Bubba Smith, an NFL athlete, was the guest star in the role of Lucius Franklin.

"ELEGANT IGGY"

Episode #86

Synopsis: Elaine hesitantly agrees to attend a classical music concert with Reverend Jim after he is given two free tickets. Elaine is pleasantly surprised when he arrives at the concert in formal attire. Elaine then introduces Jim to an art patron, Mrs. Weber, who invites both of them to a party at her home. Fearing the worst about what Reverend Jim might say or do, Elaine asks Alex to escort her to the Webers'. Elaine then realizes that Jim's feelings will be hurt if she goes with Alex, so she decides to ask Jim to accompany her after all. At first, it appears that Jim will embarrass Elaine with some of his usual off-the-wall behavior. But he suprises her by entertaining everyone at the party with an accomplished performance on the piano. (Reverend Jim had music lessons as a child.) Jim especially impresses a beautiful woman named Lindsay.

Credits: Noam Pitlik directed the script by Ken Estin. Nina Van Pallandt played Lindsay, Fran Ryan was Mrs. Weber, and Robert Denison was Earl.

For the script of "Elegant Iggy," Ken Estin won an Emmy in 1982 for outstanding writing in an episode of a comedy series.

"THE WEDDING OF LATKA AND SIMKA"

Episode #87

Synopsis: Latka startles the cabbies by bringing Dr. Joyce Brothers to the Sunshine Garage; he informs them that she has cured him of his recent multiple-personality problems. Now that his mental health seems sound, he plans to ask for Simka's hand in marriage. The cabbies are pleased to hear this, but then Latka explains that according to the established traditions of his country, a "gewirtzal" (a type of marriage broker) must propose for him. Latka selects Alex as his gewirtzal, and Alex is very persuasive in his proposal to Simka. Simka accepts, and an elaborate wedding is planned. Many people, including Latka's mother, Greta Gravas, attend the wedding dressed in the costumes of the old country. According to tradition, Latka wears a gown and Simka is dressed like a man. The wedding is more of a test than a ceremony. At the end, Latka and Simka become man and wife.

Credits: James Burrows directed the script by Howard Gewirtz and Ian Praiser. The guest stars were Carol Kane, as Simka Dahblitz; Susan Kellermann, as Greta Gravas; Dr. Joyce Brothers, as herself; Vincent Schiavelli, as the priest; and Peter Elbling, as Mascha, an interpreter.

This episode is truly strange; most of the scenes are filled with bizarre rituals from Latka's country. The problem with episodes like "The Wedding of Latka and Simka" is that the style of humor is completely different from that of most *Taxi*

Alex plays a "Gewirtzal" in "The Wedding of Latka and Simka." *(Courtesy of Ian Praiser)*

episodes. While most of *Taxi*'s humor is based on realistic situations, the jokes in this episode are based on situations as wacky as any that we see in a Marx Brothers movie.

"COOKING FOR TWO"

Episode #88

Synopsis: Jim is eating breakfast one morning when a wrecking ball crashes through the wall of his apartment. "You put up with a few inconveniences when you live in a condemned building," he tells the other cabbies. Obviously, Jim badly needs a new place to stay, and he selects Louie as the person he'd most like to live with. Louie grudgingly lets him use his apartment for a few days. Soon after moving in, Jim accidentally sets fire to Louie's apartment; nearly everything Louie owns is destroyed. Louie is, of course, enraged and he immediately fires Jim from the cab company. The only way Jim can get his job back is by giving

Louie a blank check from his father. Since Jim's dad is a millionaire, Louie realizes that he has a chance to make a killing. (Louie is actually salivating as he examines the check.) He has a problem, though: how big an amount does he dare to fill in on the check? He knows that if he chooses too large a figure, Jim's dad may call the bank and stop payment on the check. Louie finally settles on $29,542, and Jim calls his dad and gets his OK. At the end Louie learns, to his dismay, that Jim's father would have covered a check for a lot more money.

Credits: James Burrows directed the script by Ken Estin and Sam Simon. J. Alan Thomas appeared as Jeff.

Ian Praiser explains, "We only were able to take one shot of the wrecking ball crashing through the wall of Jim's apartment; we had to just hope it all looked right the first time. It was a very elaborate setup—with everything crashing and falling inside the apartment—and we wouldn't have had time to redo it if anything had gone wrong."

There are several very funny moments in "Cooking for Two"—including the scenes in which Jim's place is wrecked (while he's oblivious to all the destruction around him) and in which Jim tries to comfort Louie after burning his apartment. Jim tells Louie, "Just keep in mind that material possessions are just excess baggage in the journey of life." Needless to say, Louie doesn't find any solace in Jim's remarks.

"THE ROAD NOT TAKEN, PART I"

Episode #89

Synopsis: Elaine is offered a job as a manager of a small art gallery in Seattle, and she considers whether she and her children should move there. While Elaine thinks things over, the other cabbies tell about moments in their lives when they had important decisions to make. Tony recalls how he may have set back his boxing career when he refused to take a dive in an important fight. Louie recalls how he first became a dispatcher for the Sunshine Cab Company. From the very first, Louie began taking bribes from the cabbies, and he gained his position through backstabbing and deceit. Jim recounts how he was first tempted into trying drugs. As a freshman at Harvard, Jim had been a model student until his girlfriend, Heather, talked him into trying a marijuana brownie. At first he resisted, saying, "The best research evidence indicates it's habit-forming and leads some people to harder drugs. And, who knows, I could be one of those people." But finally he does allow himself to be persuaded to eat a "funny" brownie—and we see that the "Reverend Jim" side of him begins to surface immediately.

Credits: James Burrows directed the script by Ken Estin and Sam Simon. Charles Cioffi was Frank; J. Pat O'Malley was Tom, the previous dispatcher for the Sunshine Cab Company; Eugene Roche was Jack; Tom Hanks was Gordon, a stoned Harvard student; and Wendy Phillips was Heather.

Some of the funniest performances in the series were given by actors or actresses appearing only briefly. For instance, Tom Hanks, who's gone on to be in such movies as *Nothing in Common*, contributes an inspired bit as a stoned college student named Gordon in Reverend Jim's segment of this episode. Gordon is so high that he picks up a hot lamp—and doesn't even realize it's too hot to handle until after he's already put it down. When he tries to say something coherent, he loses the train of his thought halfway through the sentence. For example, after Jim suggests they go study, Gordon attempts to reply to him, "Jim, don't you understand? All the studying and all the books and all the gymnasiums"—then he looks totally confused and adds, "I forgot my socks."

"THE ROAD NOT TAKEN, PART II"

Episode #90

Synopsis: While Elaine continues to consider taking the job in Seattle, the cabbies reminisce about important decisions they've made in their lives. Latka recalls the day when he left the old country to go to New York. His mother warned him that in America "they keep dogs as pets and eat chickens, and they have toilets in their houses." Still, Latka decided to seek his fortune in America. Alex tells the other cabbies a story about himself and ambition. We learn that Alex once had a chance to become the regional manager of a big company. He seemed to have an excellent chance of getting the job, except for his inability to put up with the bootlicking behavior that his superior, Mr. Ambrose, expected of him. Near the end of the episode, Mr. Thompson, from the art gallery in Seattle, comes to the garage and asks Elaine for her answer. He pressures her to make her decision at once, and Elaine becomes so flustered that she gets angry with him—and even throws a punch at him. As a result, she blows her chances of getting the job in Seattle. "You're much too emotionally high-strung for this job," Mr. Thompson says.

Credits: James Burrows directed the script by Howard Gewirtz and Ian Praiser. The guest stars were Susan Kellermann, as Greta Gravas; Max Wright, as Mr. Ambrose; Matthew Faison, as Mr. Thompson; and Melanie Gaffin and David Mendenhall, as Jennifer and Jason, Elaine's children.

FIFTH-SEASON CREDITS

Alex Rieger—Judd Hirsch
Elaine Nardo—Marilu Henner
Louie DePalma—Danny DeVito
Tony Banta—Tony Danza
Jim Ignatowski—Christopher Lloyd
Latka Gravas—Andy Kaufman
Simka Gravas—Carol Kane

Executive Producers—James Brooks, Stan Daniels, and Ed. Weinberger

Producers—Ken Estin, Sam Simon, and Richard Sakai

Executive Script Consultant—David Lloyd

Executive Story Editor—Katherine Green

Story Consultant—Al Aidekman

Associate Producer—Cary D. Matsumura

Executive Consultant—Harvey Miller

Executive Creative Consultant—James Brooks

Film Editor—M. Pam Blumenthal

Art Director—Ed La Porta

Director of Photography—Kenneth Peach

Unit Production Manager—Michael Stanislavsky

Music—Bob James

"THE SHLOOGEL SHOW"

Episode #91

Synopsis: Following a tradition from their country, Latka and Simka host a party at which Alex, Elaine, Tony, Louie, and Jim are supposed to meet their ideal mates. We see that Latka and Simka have chosen wisely, for each person they have picked out is well matched to one of the members of the *Taxi* gang. Tony's date for the evening is Vicki DeStefano, a tough-talking Italian girl who reminds Tony of his mother. Louie is matched up with Judy Griffith, a blind girl who says, "I can't tell whether you're talking this way because you realize that I can't stand

being pitied—or because you're just gross." Elaine's guy is Arnie Ross, a mild-mannered man with a history of being ineffectual with women. Jim is paired up with Marcia Wallace (playing herself) of *The Bob Newhart Show*. And Alex quickly becomes enamored of Susan McDaniels, who's both witty and beautiful. At first Susan seems not to respond at all favorably to Alex, but in the end she does give him her phone number.

Credits: Noam Pitlik directed the script by Ken Estin and Sam Simon. The guest stars were Wallace Shawn as Arnie Ross, Anne DeSalvo as Vicki DeStefano, Murphy Cross as Judy Griffith, Carlene Watkins as Susan McDaniels, and Marcia Wallace as herself.

Louie immediately hits it off with Judy, a blind girl, in "The Shloogel Show."

Most of the boyfriends and girlfriends introduced in "The Shloogel Show" returned in later episodes: Arnie Ross was in "Arnie Meets the Kids," Vicki DeStefano was in "Tony's Baby," and Judy Griffith was in "Louie and the Blind Girl." If *Taxi* had gone into a sixth season, the producers intended to bring some of these characters back again. Ian Praiser explains that "those relationships were developed to provide more continuity to the show. . . . To keep a show alive, you want to keep adapting it, making changes."

"ALEX GOES OFF THE WAGON"

Episode #92

Synopsis: Alex takes a passenger to Atlantic City; while he's there, Alex decides to try his chances at some gambling. He gets lucky and wins two thousand dollars at one of the casinos. The incident brings out the compulsive gambler in Alex, and soon he's trying to get into every game he can find. Alex keeps losing money on his gambling binge, finally becoming desperate enough to ask Reverend Jim to loan him money. Seeing that Alex is in serious trouble, Jim tells Alex a story about his own problems with compulsive behavior. (Jim's addiction was, of course, to drugs rather than gambling.) Alex then comes to his senses and puts a stop to his gambling binge.

Credits: Noam Pitlik directed the script by Dennis Kallis. Anthony Carnota ap-peared as the stickman at the crap table, and J. Alan Thomas appeared as Jeff.

"JIM'S INHERITANCE"

Episode #93

Synopsis: Reverend Jim's father dies and leaves three and a half million dollars to Jim. But Jim's brother and sister, contending that Jim is mentally incompetent to handle the money, petition a judge to name them as conservators of the estate. John Bickers, the Caldwell attorney, tells Jim, "The inheritance will be yours, but you'll be treated as a child." "That sounds pretty good to me," replies Jim. Yet the other cabbies convince him that he should fight for what is rightfully his, and the case goes before a judge. Noting that Jim has done some unusual things, such as living in an condemned building for four years, the judge rules against him and in favor of his brother and sister. In the last scene Jim gets a trunk full of stuff that his dad has left him. Included in the trunk is Mr. Caldwell's best suit. (Jim holds up the pants, which are of Brobdingnagian proportions.) Jim finds a cassette in a jacket pocket of the suit, and when he plays it he discovers a kind of farewell message from his father: the recording is of the Stevie Wonder song "You Are the Sunshine of My Life."

Credits: Noam Pitlik directed the script by Ken Estin. Dick Sargent portrayed Bickers and F. William Parker appeared as the judge.

Latka and Simka wait for fate to decide which cabbie will go to bed with Simka in "Sceneskees from a Marriage."

"SCENESKEES FROM A MARRIAGE, PART I"

Episode #94

Synopsis: Latka goes out to rescue a female cabbie who's stuck in a snowstorm. He reaches her, but his tow truck breaks down. Latka and the girl, whose name is Cindy, find themselves about to be frozen to death in her cab. In order to stay warm, they realize the only thing they can do is to make love. Cindy says, "It's a very simple choice. Either you have sex with me, or you freeze to death." He agrees with her reasoning, they make love, and they survive long enough to be rescued by the state police. When Latka comes home to Simka, she takes one look at him and immediately says, "You did it with another woman." She insists they go to an old-country priest, Reverend Gorky, for counseling and advice. Latka confesses his sin. "I have been unfaithful to my wife and a disgrace to my family," Latka tells the priest. Reverend Gorky then decrees that Simka can atone for Latka's indiscretion if she will sleep with one of Latka's coworkers at the garage.

Credits: Noam Pitlik directed the script by Ian Praiser and Howard Gewirtz. The guest star was Vincent Schiavelli, as Reverend Gorky. Allyce Beasley played Cindy, Peter Elbling played Mascha, the interpreter, and J. Alan Thomas played Jeff, the assistant dispatcher.

Allyce Beasley, who plays Cindy in this episode, is currently featured as Ms. Dipesto on the hit ABC series *Moonlighting.*

"SCENESKEES FROM A MARRIAGE, PART II"

Episode #95

Synopsis: Latka and Simka's priest has ruled that Simka must sleep with someone Latka works with. They can't decide which cabbie she should choose, so they decide to have a dinner party—the last man to arrive will be the one to go to bed with her. Simka says to Latka, "It is impossible for either of us to pick. We will let the fates decide." It turns out that Alex is the last to arrive (much to Simka's relief, because she was afraid it would be Louie). Later, Simka goes to Alex's apartment and lets him know she expects them to sleep together; if he refuses, Simka explains, she and Latka will have to be divorced. "I suppose you want someone to talk to," Alex says to her. "Talk is cheap," she replies. "I want your body." Yet Alex refuses to go through with it, and Latka and Simka are divorced. Later, they are feeling terribly depressed because their marriage is over. Reverend Jim then suggests, "Why don't they just get married again?" Alex tells Jim, "It's not that simple. Do you think they'd go through this hell if they could just get married again?" But apparently this incredibly obvious suggestion hasn't occured to Latka or Simka, for as soon as they hear it, they rush off to the priest in order to be remarried.

Credits: Noam Pitlik directed the script by Ian Praiser and Howard Gewirtz.

This is one of the few episodes in which someone mentions that Alex is Jewish. Although it seems obvious throughout the series that Alex must come from a Jewish family, it's rarely talked about. In "Sceneskees from a Marriage, Part II," when Simka asks Alex to sleep with her, he says, "That's barbaric. Are you telling me that in that religion of yours, two wrongs actually make a right?" To which Simka replies sarcastically, "'In that religion of yours?' Do you mock us? Do I mock you because you do not eat animals with cloven hooves unless they chew their cud?"

"ALEX THE GOFER"

Episode #96

Synopsis: Two Broadway producers hail Alex's cab one day, and he gets into a conversation with them. We learn that Alex knows quite a lot about the theater and that Alex wanted to work in the theater when he was younger. "I'd have done anything just to get my foot in the door," he says. The producers tell him they're interviewing for gofers the next day. "It's too bad you're not twenty years younger," one of them comments. Later, Alex tells the gang about his conversation with the producers, and the other cabbies persuade him to apply for the job as a gofer. Alex is hired, but the job turns out to be extremely demeaning. He's forced to do the most petty kinds of tasks. He blows up seat cushions. He has to go through garbage looking for a lost watch. At one point Alex makes an intelligent suggestion to a producer about how to handle a scene, and the producer replies, "I don't want to sound rude—but we'll save the living theater, you take care of the patty melts." Alex has nearly had enough and is about to quit when the producer comes back and tells him they'll try his suggestion after all.

Credits: Michael Lessac directed the script by David Lloyd. The guest stars were Matthew Lawrence as Allen and David Palmer as Ned.

A good sign that Alex is being mistreated by the theatrical producers is that he lets Louie, of all people, give him some advice. When he sees the depths that Alex has sunk to, Louie asks, "Do you know what was special about you? You knew you were nothing, but you were great at it." Louie convinces Alex that he ought to quit being a gofer. (Yet just a few minutes later Alex learns that the producers will use one of his ideas in their production.)

"LOUIE'S REVENGE"

Episode #97

Synopsis: Louie finds out that Emily, a beautiful photographer, has just broken up with her latest boyfriend. When Louie dated Emily in the past, he admits to the cabbies, she was always able to twist him around her finger; now Louie's determined to get even with her for the way she treated him before. "When she called me 'gross and disgusting,' I had a drink in my hand," Louie remembers. "I always regretted that I didn't throw it in her face." Yet when Louie sees Emily this time, he falls for her all over again. He becomes obsessed by her, and she has him running errands for her all over town. Furthermore, she won't even allow herself to be seen in public with him. Louie begs Alex for help. "Don't let me become a weenie," he says to Alex. Eventually, though, Louie finds the courage to tell Emily off. "You know something,

In "Louie's Revenge," Louie gets involved with Emily, who is able to twist him around her finger.

Emily? Someday your Mr. Right is gonna come along. And when he does he's gonna be wearin' a white coat and carryin' a butterfly net.''

Credits: Stan Daniels directed the script by Sam Simon. Andrea Marcovicci was the guest star as Emily.

One especially good moment from "Louie's Revenge" occurs when Louie wakes up in bed with Emily. From the way he looks at her face while she's asleep, we can tell he is really smitten by her. But when she awakens and sees his face, she screams.

"TRAVELS WITH MY DAD"

Episode #98

Synopsis: Tony's father, Angelo, a merchant seaman, comes to New York to visit his son. Angelo brings along a surprise— a union card that will permit Tony to join him on his next ocean voyage. As a boy, Tony had dreamed of a life at sea, but he hesitates to take his father up on his offer to become a merchant seaman. Tony decides to give the job a try, though, and he travels with his father on a month-long trip to Singapore. (In Singapore, Tony and his dad get into a brawl at a bar, and they wind up in a tattoo parlor.) Tony discovers he's not really cut out to follow in his father's footsteps, however; he spends most of the voyage being seasick.

Credits: Michael Zinberg directed the script by Barton Dean. Donnelly Rhodes portrayed Angelo Banta, Dick Miller was Fergie, and Wendell Wright was Sam.

"We had a hell of a bar fight in 'Travels with My Dad,'" says Michael Zinberg, who directed this episode. "We shot the fight once in the afternoon and once again in the evening that Friday. . . . When we had a gag or a special effect that we wanted to be sure we got right, sometimes we would shoot it in the afternoon, too."

"ELAINE AND THE MONK"

Episode #99

Synopsis: Simka's cousin Zifka is a monk from the old country. His monastic order permits him to indulge in worldly pleasures for only one week every ten years. On a visit to New York during one of those weeks, he takes an immediate interest in Elaine, who's intrigued by the idea of dating a monk. (At one point she comments, "Here I am in the same old rut, going dancing with a monk.") They have some good times together—on one occasion they dance to "Cheek to Cheek"—and succeed in making Alex jealous of Zifka. Alex accuses Elaine of toying with Zifka's affections. But Elaine

and Zifka's romance seems to be progressing well—until the week abruptly come to an end. Immediately, Zifka falls silent and, as his monastic vows require, leaves Elaine's apartment without further ado.

Credits: Danny DeVito directed the script by David Lloyd. Mark Blankfield was the guest star as Zifka.

The dance sequence in this episode was choreographed by Debbie Allen, who recently starred on Broadway in the musical *Sweet Charity.* "Elaine and the Monk" is also noteworthy because it marked the

Simka's cousin Zifka turns out to be a surprisingly good dancer in "Elaine and the Monk."

first time that Danny DeVito directed an episode of *Taxi*. (He has since directed episodes of the series *Mary*, starring Mary Tyler Moore, as well as the made-for-TV movie *The Ratings Game*.)

was the guest star as Zena. Peter Jurasik portrayed Tom Pelton, Robert Moberly portayed a waiter, Patrick Davis was "Gramps," and Jim Pollack was the man at the table in the French restaurant.

"ZENA'S HONEYMOON"

Episode #100

Synopsis: Zena Sherman, who had been Louie's girlfriend, visits the garage and asks to see Louie again. At dinner Louie tells her, "The door is open, Zena. You've suffered enough. Come in out of the rain." But while Louie wants to get back together with Zena, she reveals to him her plans for getting married to somebody else—and she invites him to the wedding. Louie is stunned by the news. He asks her, "Who is he? Who's the guy? Who's the next victim?" With his usual tact Louie then suggests, "Wouldn't you at least have the decency to go to bed with me one last time?" After refusing to attend the wedding, Louie decides to invite himself along on the ship where Zena and Tom Pelton, a child psychiatrist, are beginning their honeymoon. Louie goes to Tom and Zena's room, where he makes a complete fool of himself—at one point he even tries to strangle Tom. With his hands on Tom's throat, Louie asks him, "Tell me why I'm doin' this, doc." As he leaves Tom and Zena, Louie says to her, "You were the best woman I ever had. And I let you go."

Credits: Richard Sakai directed the script by David Lloyd. Rhea Perlman

"LOUIE MOVES UPTOWN"

Episode #101

Synopsis: Elaine suggests that Louie move out of his dump and into a better apartment. He considers her advice and goes to look at an apartment in an exclusive building that is so classy "even the doorbell has a British accent." He loves the plush co-op apartment, but he doesn't have enough money for the down payment. Louie then turns to Jim: "Jim, I know they say that money can't buy love. But if you give me these forty-eight big ones, it'll be Valentine's Day forever." Jim loans Louie the money, and Louie next faces one last hurdle: he must be approved by the co-op board. The members of the board are so stuffy they turn down Penny Marshall (playing herself) as a buyer; they say they disapprove of the life-style of performers. Louie manages to impress the pompous members of the board favorably, though, by telling them just what they want to hear and by playing the part of someone as snobbish as they are. Alex goes with him to the interview and is disgusted at the board's behavior. Louie is not, and Alex says that it is appropriate that he live there: they deserve each other.

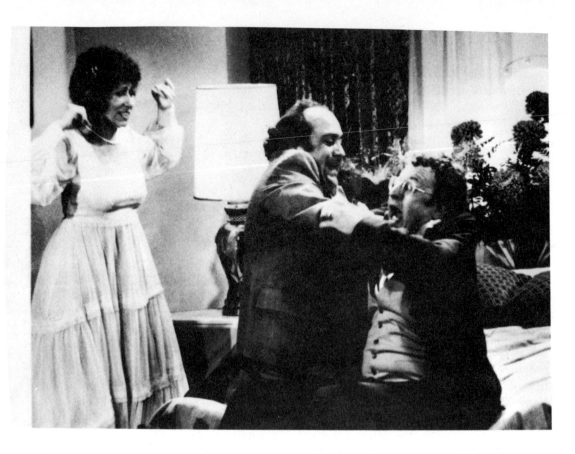

"Tell me why I'm doin' this, doc," Louie asks Tom Pelton, a child psychiatrist, as he tries to strangle him in "Zena's Honeymoon."

Credits: Michael Zinberg directed the script by David Lloyd. Penny Marshall appeared as a would-be buyer.

In this episode a serious subject—discrimination—is tackled, and it is handled very well. On *Taxi* when a controversial subject is brought up, it's always handled in a very entertaining way—we don't sense that the producers are trying to make some kind of a heavy-handed "statement."

An especially funny scene is the one in which Penny Marshall (playing herself) comes to apply to live in the exclusive apartment building. After being told that "we wouldn't allow an actor to live here, even if he were English," she makes a gesture on behalf of the dignity of her profession: she "moons" the stuffy members of the co-op board.

"CRIME AND PUNISHMENT"

Episode #102

Synopsis: Mr. Ratledge, the current owner of the Sunshine Cab Company, discovers that somebody from the garage has been secretly selling off used auto parts and keeping the money for himself. Mr. Ratledge orders Louie to find out who the thief is—and fire him. Since Louie is in fact the crook, he talks Jeff into taking the blame, assuring him that nothing serious will come of the incident. (Louie promises he will rehire Jeff after Ratledge cools down.) But Mr. Ratledge is so incensed about what has happened that he decides to press criminal charges against Jeff. Jeff is taken to the police station, where Alex posts bail to have him released. Jeff has finally had enough, and he demands that Louie tell Mr. Ratledge the truth. Louie then admits he's the thief, but Ratledge refuses to believe him—he thinks that Louie is covering for Jeff. In the end, Ratledge says that since Louie seems to be so deeply worried about Jeff's fate, he'll agree to drop all the charges against him and give him his job back as assistant dispatcher. Louie gloats over how he has committed a series of crimes and has gotten off scot-free.

Credits: Stan Daniels directed the script by Katherine Green. Allen Goorwitz was the guest star, in the role of Mr. Ratledge. J. Alan Thomas portrayed Jeff.

Louie is really gleeful when he discovers he's gotten away with stealing. "Let's face it, Rieger," Louie says, "crime pays." And Alex is thoroughly appalled at Louie's lack of any sense of guilt

In "Crime and Punishment," Jeff gets sent to jail for a crime that Louie committed.

over what he has done. Both Danny DeVito's and Judd Hirsch's performances are excellent in this episode.

"GET ME THROUGH THE HOLIDAYS"

Episode #103

Synopsis: Alex's plans to work instead of celebrating Christmas are affected when his ex-wife Phyllis shows up and asks him to help her out of the holiday blues. She pleads with him to allow her to stay in his apartment for a few days. Alex even takes her along in his cab at one point, and later he brings her to a Christmas party at Latka and Simka's place, where Phyllis depresses everyone with her surly remarks. After the party Phyllis tells Alex that her Christmas present to him is that she will be leaving town soon.

Credits: Michael Zinberg directed the script by Ken Estin and Sam Simon. Louise Lasser was the guest star as Phyllis.

"ALEX'S OLD BUDDY"

Episode #104

Synopsis: Alex is reunited with his pet dog Buddy, but we see that the dog is no longer in the best of health. (After all, Buddy is nineteen years old.) A veterinarian tells Alex that his dog has only a few more weeks to live, and Alex becomes determined to make Buddy as happy as possible during the time he has left. Instead of dog food, Alex feeds Buddy steaks. Alex even takes Buddy along in his cab, although Louie objects, suggesting instead that Buddy be put to sleep. "He's a hound of hell, he's a devil dog," says Louie. Eventually, Alex has to take Buddy back to the vet's, where the dog dies. At the end of the episode we see Alex crying over Buddy.

Credits: Richard Sakai directed the script by Ken Estin and Sam Simon. John Hancock portrayed Dr. Brandon, the vet; Judith-Marie Bergan portrayed Alex's friend Shawn; and "Tucker" was Alex's dog Buddy.

Alex learns that his pet dog has only a few weeks to live in "Alex's Old Buddy."

"SUGAR RAY NARDO"

Episode #105

Synopsis: Elaine's son, Jason, is fed up with his oboe lessons and wants instead to take up boxing. Tony invites Jason to come to the gym and join the boys' boxing program (in which large, heavily padded gloves are used). Jason pleads with his mother to let him fight; he shrewdly tells her that his dad would have allowed it. Not wanting to be overprotective, Elaine gives in. She explains to Alex, "I'm afraid that Jason's missing out on something by being raised by a single mother." Yet Elaine soon wishes she hadn't let Jason box, since he gets his nose broken in his first fight.

Credits: Danny DeVito directed the script by Katherine Green. The guest star was David Mendenhall, portraying Jason.

Katherine Green, the writer of "Sugar Ray Nardo," explains, "I had a sister who was at that time trying to raise a son, and she had gone through the same kind of situation as in this episode. What happens in these situations is that the kid will say to his mother, 'If daddy were here, he would let me play football'—or box, or whatever."

"ALEX GETS BURNED BY AN OLD FLAME"

Episode #106

Synopsis: A lovely ex-girlfriend of Jim's, Diane MacKenna, shows up at the Sunshine Cab Company. (She had once lived with Jim on a commune.) Alex is immediately intrigued by Diane, who is now a lawyer. Alex says to her, "You get to save people's lives. The only thing I do for my fellow men is get them to the airport on time." Though Alex is plainly attracted to Diane, she tells him she's still "emotionally and physically involved" with Jim. Alex is naturally surprised to hear this, and he tells Diane he wouldn't think she'd be interested in a "flake" like Jim. Later, Jim comes over to Alex's apartment, angry that Alex has insulted him. But after Alex points out some of the bizarre things Jim has done, such as

living in a condemned building for four years, even Jim has to agree that he is a flake.

Credits: Harvey Miller directed the script by Barton Dean. Cathie Shirriff was the guest star, in the role of Diane MacKenna. Martin Azarow played the part of Leon and Robert Moberly played the part of a waiter.

"TONY'S BABY"

Episode #107

Synopsis: Tony's girlfriend Vicki (who was introduced in "The Shloogel Show") informs him that she is pregnant. He's stunned by her revelation and asks her to marry him. At first, she refuses—she thinks he's only proposing because he feels obligated to. Tony is scheduled to fight a major contender, the tenth-ranked middleweight in the world, at Madison Square Garden, yet he is so worried about Vicki that he can't concentrate on his boxing. He admits to his new manager, Leo Goodman, and to Alex that he doesn't care whether he wins or loses. Tony is defeated in his fight, but afterwards Vicki agrees to marry him. At the end of the episode, though, Tony still seems to be debating whether or not he should marry her.

Credits: Richard Sakai directed the script by Dari Daniels. The guest star, in the role of Vicki, was Anne DeSalvo. Keenan Wynn (well known for his performances in many films, including *Dr. Strangelove*) played Leo Goodman, while

James F. Lennon was the announcer and Gene LeBell was the referee.

"We went through lots of rewrites on that episode," remembers Katherine Green, who was the executive story editor during the last season of *Taxi*. "We couldn't decide whether we wanted Tony to get married. So we finally left it open at the end. . . . There did seem to be a good rapport between Tony and the girl, though. Lots of people felt they looked cute together."

"JIM'S MARIO'S"

Episode #108

Synopsis: Jim invests some of his inheritance by purchasing Mario's. Reverend Jim is happy with his decision, but Mario's is actually a bad investment: it's been losing money for years. Jim's brother Tom comes to look at the restaurant, and he pronounces it "the sleaziest dive I've ever seen. . . . Jim, you've squandered your money. You're an immature, irresponsible, childlike simpleton." Tom tells Jim that in the future he won't trust him with large sums of money. But Jim asks his brother to come back in one week; by then he hopes business at Mario's will be better. To help Jim, the other cabbies work hard to bring as many customers as possible to Mario's. When Tom returns a week later, he sees that Mario's has become successful after all.

Credits: Danny DeVito directed the script by Ken Estin and Sam Simon. Walter Olkewicz played Tom Caldwell, T. J. Castronova played Tommy, Charles Bouvier was a customer at Mario's, and Sharon Madden was a nun.

In "Jim's Mario's" there's an amusing subplot about an inspector from the liquor commission. He tries to shut Mario's down by posing as a customer who wants to buy a bottle after hours. Jim gives him a bottle in a bag, and the man reveals his true identity. At this moment it looks as if Jim is in serious trouble, but he shows the inspector that the bottle he has given him is really full of club soda, instead of booze.

"LOUIE AND THE BLIND GIRL"

Episode #109

Synopsis: Louie is in love with Judy, a blind girl (whom we first met in "The Shloogel Show"), and he plans to give her a diamond ring and ask her to marry him. But he loses his courage when he learns that she is going to have an operation that will restore her sight. Louie's afraid—and not without some cause, it must be admitted—that Judy will not consider him to be dashingly handsome. "Louie, you're much too insecure about your appearance," Alex says. With some prodding from Alex, Louie agrees to go to the hospital to visit Judy after her operation. Louie is dismayed to find that her doctor is tall, young, and handsome. Still, Louie resolves to be at her bedside when Judy's

Louie is afraid that Judy won't love him if an operation restores her sight in "Louie and the Blind Girl."

bandages are removed, so that he'll be the first person she sees. Louie is relieved when she doesn't mind his looks at all.

Credits: Noam Pitlik directed the script by Larry Anderson. Murphy Cross was the guest star as Judy. David Young appeared as Dr. Gordon.

Katherine Green explains that the producers didn't have any definite plans about what would have happened to Louie and Judy if the show had gone into a sixth season. "You don't really think ahead very far with these characters," Katherine Green says. "You bring someone into a series and see how they work: we didn't have a master plan about what would be happening in the future. Besides, it could turn out that the actor or actress we had planned to turn into a regular simply wouldn't be available during the next year."

"SIMKA'S MONTHLIES"

Episode #110

Synopsis: Simka fails to show up for several appointments at the Immigration Department, and she is in serious danger of being deported. We discover that the reason she hasn't been going to the interviews is because she is suffering from some sort of medical problem that causes her moods to shift violently from one extreme to another. Jim correctly diagnoses her illness as premenstrual syndrome. "I read about it in the *Harvard Medical Journal*," Jim says. "Or was it on a box of Cocoa Puffs?" Alex and Elaine convince Simka that her condition can be treated. Simka gets medical help, but when she and Latka go to an interview at the Immigration Department, an official tells them that he thinks they have merely a "paper marriage" in order to avoid deportation. Simka and Latka are saved, though, when the official sees them quarreling so fiercely that he says, "I'm fully convinced now that you're genuinely man and wife."

Credits: Harvey Miller directed the script by Holly Holmberg Brooks. The Immigration officer was played by Howard Witt.

"The idea for this episode came from Holly Holmberg Brooks" (James Brooks's wife), remembers Katherine Green. "Doing a show about premenstrual syndrome was very unusual for a sitcom, and it was a tough topic to make funny. Holly felt that women should know that large numbers of other women are also suffering from this problem."

"ARNIE MEETS THE KIDS"

Episode #111

Synopsis: Elaine's relationship with Arnie Ross (who was introduced in "The Shloogel Show") has reached a point where she decides it's time that he should meet her children, Jason and Jennifer. Arnie is extremely anxious about making a good impression on them. When he arrives at Elaine's apartment, he does everything he can think of to entertain the kids. He blows up balloon animals. He amuses the kids with hand puppets. And when he finally does run out of entertaining things to do, Jennifer asks him, "What's next?" For a second Arnie is at a loss. "Next?" he wonders. Then he reaches into his jacket and says, "How about—money!" Then he begins doling out twenty-dollar bills to the kids. (They are ecstatic when they take the cash.) Elaine won't stand for this, though, and she forces Jason and Jennifer to give Arnie back his money. Still, the rest of the evening goes pretty well. After the children go to bed, Arnie sees that Elaine is worried about something. He quickly discerns the problem. "In other words," Arnie says to Elaine, "you don't really know quite where our relationship is going, and you don't really know quite how you feel about me. So the fact that your kids like me might make it more difficult to break up." But we learn that Elaine does want to continue seeing Arnie. "You're such a dear man," she tells him. "I'm glad you think so," responds Arnie. "Because now you may be stuck with me."

Credits: Richard Sakai directed the

script by John Markus. Wallace Shawn was the guest star, in the role of Arnie Ross. David Mendenhall played Jason, Melanie Gaffin played Jennifer, and Wendy Jewell played a woman cab driver.

Who could be more anxious than Arnie Ross? Arnie gets as nervous about the simple matter of meeting Elaine's kids as most people would get if they were to meet an ax murderer in a dark alley. Seeing that Arnie is extremely ill at ease with Jason and Jennifer, Elaine asks, "Arnie, would you like to take off your coat?" "Are you kidding?" Arnie replies. "I'm fighting for my life here."

"A GRAND GESTURE"

Episode #112

Synopsis: We learn that Jim has been giving away large amounts of money to strangers. When Alex finds out, he tells Jim that his behavior is reckless and irresponsible. Alex even threatens to call the administrators of the Caldwell estate. In defense of what he's been doing, Jim says he gives the money away for the thrill of seeing the expressions on people's faces when they receive a completely unexpected gift. To make his point with everyone in the garage, Jim gives a thousand dollars apiece to Tony, Alex, Elaine, Latka, and Louie, for each of them to give away. Jim feels confident that if they experience the thrill of giving, they won't think his actions are irresponsible—and it turns out that the other cabbies do

agree with him afterwards. Tony uses his money to buy a giant TV for Walt, an eccentric old black man whose only pleasure is watching television. Alex plans to give his thousand dollars to the next guy who gets into his cab with a hard-luck story. But after considering a would-be political cartoonist (who turns out to have no talent), Alex says he gave the money to a woman and her children who were about to be evicted. Elaine gives her money to her daughter, Jennifer. Latka's thousand dollars goes to his minister, Reverend Gorky, who in turn gives it to Simka so that she and Latka can afford to have a baby. And Louie gives his money to Jeff, who only very reluctantly accepts it. "All I know is that if it comes from Louie DePalma, there's got to be a catch," he says. Finally, though, Louie convinces him otherwise.

Credits: Noam Pitlik directed the script by Ken Estin and Sam Simon. The guest stars were J. Alan Thomas as Jeff, Vincent Schiavelli as Reverend Gorky, Tracey Walter as the bum that Jim gives money to, Tom Villard as Jeremy, Melanie Gaffin as Jennifer, and Scatman Crothers as Walt.

"A Grand Gesture" wound up as the last episode of *Taxi* to feature any new material. (Episodes #113 and #114, "*Taxi* Retrospective, Parts I and II," were made up exclusively of clips from old episodes.) Ian Praiser comments, "Even at that point [near the end of the fifth season], there was still hope that the show would be picked up again. No one wanted to do a final episode, because that would have been admitting, 'This is indeed the end.'"

"*TAXI* RETROSPECTIVE, PART I"

Episode #113

Synopsis: This episode is made up of highlights from "Like Father, Like Daughter," "Paper Marriage," "Reverend Jim: A Space Odyssey," "Blind Date," "Elaine's Strange Triangle," and "Sceneskees from a Marriage."

Unlike many other successful series, *Taxi* had no real final episode—only this "retrospective" of old clips, which was originally broadcast as a one-hour special. "It wouldn't have been right for the series to have had a final episode to tie up loose ends, the way they did with *M*A*S*H* or *Mary Tyler Moore*," says Ian Praiser. "In real life everyone's good or bad luck doesn't happen at the same time. . . . It would have been much too convenient if everybody's own dream came true in one episode. Even if the cab company had gone broke, the drivers would've only gone on to another cab company. And so the story would've continued."

"*TAXI* RETROSPECTIVE, PART II"

Episode #114

Synopsis: This episode is made up of highlights from "Memories of Cab 804," "Louie and the Nice Girl," "Elegant Iggy," "Jim the Psychic," and "Fantasy Borough."

EPILOGUE—WHAT THE PEOPLE WHO MADE *TAXI* HAVE BEEN DOING RECENTLY

Many of the people involved with the show have recently gone on to other successes. *Taxi* has made a star out of nearly everyone in the cast, and most of the producers, writers, and directors have worked on other hit series in the past few years.

James Brooks wrote and directed *Terms of Endearment*, a critically acclaimed picture that was one of the top moneymakers of 1984. Fans of *Taxi* will notice that the film has a lot in common with Brooks's TV shows. We recognize the same mixture of comedy and pain in both—and the same emphasis on coping with everyday problems. Even though *Terms of Endearment* ends with the death of the Debra Winger character, there are many scenes, especially those with Jack

Nicholson, that could have been taken straight out of a sitcom.

Brooks's next film, which he will again both write and direct, will feature William Hurt, Holly Hunger, and Albert Brooks. It will be released in late 1987 or early 1988.

One of the creators of *The Cosby Show*, the top-rated series on TV now, was Ed. Weinberger. Along with Stan Daniels, Weinberger also created *The Associates*, a series that starred Wilfrid Hyde-White. Plus, Daniels and Weinberger wrote the script for the highly amusing movie *The Lonely Guy* (1984), starring Steve Martin.

Many of the people involved with the hit NBC series *Cheers* are veterans of *Taxi*. *Cheers* was created by James Burrows (who has also directed many episodes of the show), Glen Charles, and Les Charles. David Lloyd has been a story

Marilu Henner's smashing good looks and well-developed figure have been showcased in such recent movies as *Perfect.*

editor for *Cheers*, and Katherine Green has been a writer for the show. Danny DeVito has been a guest star. And Rhea Perlman has won three Emmies for her role.

The credits for *All Is Forgiven*, a sitcom that lasted for only nine weeks on NBC despite Nielsen ratings among the top ten shows, were filled with names familiar to *Taxi* viewers. Carol Kane was one of the stars of the show, and Howard Gewirtz, Ian Praiser, James Burrows, Glen Charles, and Les Charles were among the producers and writers.

Another former *Taxi* writer who's doing very well for himself these days is Barry Kemp, the executive producer and creator of the sitcom *Newhart*. He's also the executive producer of the miniseries *Fresno.*

Michael Zinberg recently was a producer for the ABC series *Heart of the City*. He has also directed some episodes of *Who's the Boss?*

Since appearing in *Taxi*, Judd Hirsch's most important role has been in the hit Broadway comedy *I'm Not Rappaport*, written by Herb Gardner. Hirsch won the Tony Award for the best actor of 1985 for his portrayal of an irascible old man in *Rappaport*. And the wonderful chemistry between Hirsch's character and the character played by Cleavon Little helped to make *I'm Not Rappaport* the Tony Award winner for best play of the year. Hirsch appeared in *Rappaport* at the Booth Theater on Broadway for most of 1985 and 1986, and in 1987 he is appearing in the national touring version of the play.

Hirsch has made several movies since *Ordinary People*, but he says he's not fully satisfied with any of them. It's true that the scripts of *Without a Trace, Brotherly Love,* and *The Good-bye People* were all fairly pedestrian efforts. Yet Hirsch contributes solid performances to all of these films, especially *Without a Trace*. Unfortunately, movie producers so far haven't offered him the really first-rate starring vehicle he deserves. Hirsch says (though it's hard to know whether or not he's joking) that he especially wants to appear as the star of an action/adventure movie like *Raiders of the Lost Ark*. He also says he would consider performing in another TV series if he were presented with a script that was good enough.

Movie producers seem to have decided that Marilu Henner is best suited to play

Danny DeVito's movie career really took off with his appearance in *Romancing the Stone.*

the part of a sex bomb. Marilu's smashing good looks and well-developed figure have been showcased in the recent movies *Rustler's Rhapsody, The Man Who Loved Women, Cannonball Run II, Love with a Perfect Stranger, Hammett, Johnny Dangerously, Stark,* and *Perfect.* Yet since *Taxi* she hasn't had much opportunity, except in the Jules Feiffer play *Grown-ups,* and the Andrew Bergman play *Social Security,* to let audiences see more of her versatility as an actress. She says, "I'd like to do a romantic comedy, a relationship kind of movie." And Marilu's fans from *Taxi* certainly hope she lands that sort of part.

Marilu Henner has also been the subject of innumerable stories in the gossip columns for her on-again, off-again ro-

mance with John Travolta, which began when they first met in 1972. She was married for a while, from 1980 to 1982, to Frederic Forrest, the actor who starred in the movie *The Rose.* Marilu frequently denies that she and Travolta have any plans to be married. "We like things the way they are," she says.

The busiest member of the cast of *Taxi* during the past few years has got to be Danny DeVito. After years of paying his dues in the early seventies, when he had trouble finding good parts, DeVito seems to be working very regularly today. He's appeared in several popular movies recently (in parts that are similar in many ways to the character of Louie DePalma), including *Romancing the Stone, The Jewel*

Tony Danza and his co-stars Judith Light and Katherine Helmond in a scene from the hit series *Who's the Boss?*

of the Nile, Ruthless People, Tin Men, and *Wise Guys.* Here is what Pauline Kael, the well-known movie critic for *The New Yorker,* had to say about his performance in *Wise Guys:* "DeVito uses his short frame confidently, assertively. . . . DeVito is controlled and resourceful, and at times he manages to be touching without any hint of pathos."

Besides his recent work as an actor, DeVito has found time to do some directing, too. (Viewers will recall that he directed three episodes of *Taxi.*) DeVito has directed several episodes of *Mary,* a sitcom from the 1985–86 season that starred Mary Tyler Moore. DeVito also directed and starred in *The Ratings Game,* a film made for The Movie Channel in 1984,

and he directed and starred in an excellent 1986 episode of NBC's *Amazing Stories.* He says he wants to do more directing, especially for feature films. "In television, particularly in three- or four-camera sitcoms," explains DeVito, "it's the producer, not the director, who's really in charge of things. That's why I want to direct movies."

DeVito's co-star in *The Ratings Game* and *Amazing Stories* was his wife, Rhea Perlman. They were married in 1981 on a lunch break from *Taxi,* and they have two children, Lucy and Gracie.

Tony Danza has received considerable publicity for his starring performance in the hit series *Who's the Boss?* on ABC and for his marriage in 1986 to Tracey Robin-

One of Christopher Lloyd's recent credits was for his performance in *The Legend of the Lone Ranger*.

Rosenberg, a small-time Brooklyn hood who is convicted of murder but who becomes a lawyer while still behind bars.

Some of Christopher Lloyd's recent credits have been for his portrayals in *Back to the Future, Star Trek III* (Reverend Jim would have been pleased about that), *The Adventures of Buckaroo Banzai, Mr. Mom, The Legend of the Lone Ranger, To Be or Not to Be,* and *Clue*. (Quite a few of those movie roles have much in common with Jim Ignatowski: Lloyd usually plays characters with more than their share of eccentricities.) Christopher Lloyd has recently been in the enviable position, due to the popularity of *Back to*

son. And he has received some unwanted publicity for his sentence in 1984 by a New York judge to serve 250 days of community service for assaulting a guard in a Manhattan restaurant.

Danza has been in several movies lately (including *Going Ape!, Murder Can Hurt You,* and *Cannonball Run II*), although none of those pictures was of a caliber likely to change the course of Western civilization. "In most of my movies, my co-star has usually been a monkey," Danza says. But in 1986 Danza got a more substantial part in the made-for-TV movie *Doing Life,* in which he plays Jerry

Jeff Conaway portrayed the dashing Prince Erik Greystone in the short-lived series *Wizards and Warriors.*

Andy Kaufman played Armageddon T. Thunderbird in the film *In God We Trust.*

Heartbeeps (with Bernadette Peters) and *In God We Trust* (with Marty Feldman). In January 1984 Kaufman learned that he had lung cancer, and he died in May 1984. Kaufman fans who would like to know more about him and about his illness should read the fine profile of Kaufman written for the November 1984 issue of *Esquire* by Elayne Boosler, who was his girlfriend and who is well known herself as a stand-up comedienne.

Carol Kane has been active lately in a variety of roles. She has been in several movies, including *Over the Brooklyn Bridge, Norman Loves Rose, The Secret Life of Sigmund Freud*, and *Jumpin' Jack Flash;* her latest movie is *Ishtar,* in which

the Future, of being flooded with offers for parts in upcoming movie projects. In 1987 Lloyd will appear in the films *Bobo the Dog Boy* (with Howie Mandel) and *White Dragon.*

Most recently Jeff Conaway has been a guest star on several television programs, such as *Murder, She Wrote, Tales from the Darkside,* and *Who's the Boss?* Conaway left *Taxi* in 1981 to be in the movie *Models.* He has also been featured in the short-lived TV series *Wizards and Warriors* on CBS in 1983 and in a Broadway production of a rock musical, entitled *The News,* in 1986.

Andy Kaufman made two movies,

One of Carol Kane's many movie roles was in *The World's Greatest Lover.*

she appears with Dustin Hoffman. Also, Carol has received some highly complimentary notices for her performance as one of the stars of the short-lived NBC series *All Is Forgiven:* she played a soap-opera writer with a Southern accent. (Don Merrill, the reviewer for *TV Guide,* called her "delightful" in the show.) Carol explains that before *Taxi* she had been known mainly for dramas and that today most of her offers are for comedies. "The path my career has taken is certainly not something I decided on," she says. "When I took the role on *Taxi* in 1981, it pretty much changed my life."

It's quite a tribute to the high quality of the cast and the producers of *Taxi* that they have been involved in such a large number of important projects in the past few years. Yet no matter what other notable movies and series they work on in the future—and it seems a sure bet that they will do many excellent things—*Taxi* will always remain one of the high points of their careers.